The View From Mars Hill

Cowley Publications is a ministry of the brothers of the Society of Saint John the Evangelist, a monastic order in the Episcopal Church. Our mission is to provide books and resources for those seeking spiritual and theological formation. Cowley Publications is committed to developing a new generation of writers and teachers who will encourage people to think and pray in new ways about spirituality, reconciliation, and the future.

The View From Mars Hill

CHRISTIANITY IN THE LANDSCAPE
OF WORLD RELIGIONS

Charles B. Jones

Cowley Publications
Cambridge, Massachusetts

Library of Congress Cataloging-in-Publication Data:
Jones, Charles Brewer, 1957-
    The view from Mars Hill : Christianity in the landscape of world religions / Charles B. Jones.
        p. cm.
Includes bibliographical references (p.   ).
    ISBN 1-56101-225-4 (pbk. : alk. paper)
    1. Christianity and other religions. 2. Church history. I. Title.
BR127.J59 2005
261.2—dc22

                                                              2005003807

Cover design: Gary Ragaglia
Text design: Lindy Gifford

This book was printed in the United States of America on acid-free paper.

Cowley Publications
4 Brattle Street
Cambridge, Massachusetts 02138
800-225-1534 • www.cowley.org

To my family, Brenda, Chenoa, and Trevor—
Three cheers for each of you!

To the congregation at St. Andrew's Episcopal Church,
College Park, Maryland, and our rector, Rev. Karla M. Woggon,
in gratitude for good fellowship and good pastoring

Acknowledgments

Special thanks go to my colleague Rev. Dr. Timothy Friedrichsen for his expert comments on the sections of this book dealing with the Bible, and to Dr. William Barbieri for needed pointers on European immigration patterns. I would also like to express my appreciation to Rev. Cynthia Shelkofsky for providing the specific information on modern missionary thinking and Douglas Horton, found in chapter six. Finally, I am very grateful to my late father-in-law, Mr. William Vockery, who, shortly before he died, brought his experienced teacher's eye to the manuscript and gave many valuable suggestions.

Contents

Introduction

The Religious Scene and the Problem of Diversity

Once a week on my local National Public Radio station, Garrison Keillor tells stories of the mythical Minnesota town of Lake Wobegon. The religious life and institutions of this bucolic town feature prominently in many of the tales he spins about the lives of its ordinary people. Some of them are of Norwegian Lutheran stock and some are German Catholic, with a smattering of small fundamentalist congregations such as the Sanctified Brethren. Keillor mentions no others, and so these three groups appear to represent the extent of religious diversity in and around Lake Wobegon and surrounding Mist County.

As recently as thirty years ago, one could have justifiably considered this picture complete, at least for rural communities and small towns. In the larger cities, one would have needed to add some other groups, most notably Jews, to round it out. Other religious groups did exist, but they were in immigrant communities, largely invisible to the majority population: some Chinese and Japanese Buddhists in New York and on the west coast, some Arab Muslims in the Midwest, and so on. Will Herberg's classic work on American religion, first published in 1955, sought to capture the variety of religions in the United States in its title: *Protestant-Catholic-Jew: An Essay in American Religious Sociology*.

Today, however, things have changed considerably. One can see

minarets, lotuses, and golden domes as part of the architectural portfolio of any given town, even alongside the steeples of the Lake Wobe-
gons of this country. So how did this change come about? The 1893
World's Parliament of Religions in Chicago brought religious leaders from many countries to America to speak to an educated audience for the first time. Some of those international figures remained
in the country to propagate their faiths to mainstream American culture. Soldiers returned from the Pacific after World War II having
been exposed to a new interest in the religions of Japan, notably Zen.
The "Beat generation" of the 1950s went in search of alternative spir-
itualities and made words like *Zen* and *dharma* part of the English
language. Change accelerated during the 1960s as social and cultural
upheaval and the accompanying search for new values drew more
and more Americans to a greater awareness of other religions around
the world. Starting from the mid-twentieth century, colleges and universities responded to the growing curiosity of their students by hiring specialists in the emerging field of "history of religions," and by
making courses in world religions more available.

   Those developments made non-Western religions much more
visible to the mainstream culture, but did not necessarily make these
religions a concrete presence in people's daily lives. According to Pro-
fessor Diana Eck, director of the Pluralism Project at Harvard University, the passage of the Immigration and Naturalization Act of
1965 opened the nation's doors and inaugurated a wave of immigration, especially from Asia. That forced an awareness of other religions on ordinary citizens, who now found that their neighbors
and coworkers might well include Muslims, Sikhs, Buddhists,
Zoroastrians, and others, and that a Sikh *gurdwara* or a Buddhist
monastery might be under construction right next to their church
or synagogue.[1] The Pluralism Project Web site gives statistics on religious groups that show decisively that the old model of religious
diversity in America—Protestant, Catholic, Jew—no longer holds.[2]
The picture is both more complicated, encompassing a great many
religious traditions, and more pervasive, reaching outside the urban
and academic centers into small towns and rural areas.

Apart from such developments as these, which affect life within national borders, the rise of the global economy has also awakened awareness of other religions. Though this trend goes back as far as the trade caravans that delivered wares throughout Europe, the Middle East, and along the Silk Road into China, and accelerated during the Age of Discovery, it grew in such astonishing proportions during the twentieth century that more citizens of the western countries became involved and found themselves dealing with partners from many lands and many faiths. More college students than ever take language and culture classes as a way of preparing to participate in international trade, and the law school associated with my own university makes available courses in Islamic law to prepare lawyers for the global stage.

The *fact* of increased religious diversity is visible on all sides and perhaps does not need extensive documentation here; anyone living in a major city can look in the Yellow Pages under "Churches" and "Religious Organizations" to see its extent right where they live. Simple statistics, however, do not address the more urgent question of *meaning.* What are we, as Christians, to make of the surge in religious diversity, and how are we to respond to it? Are other religions simply wrong, and do we therefore need to increase our efforts in missions and evangelism to convert the others? Is this great multiplicity a desirable state of affairs, rather like biodiversity in the natural world, calling us to appreciate and foster it? Is there any way to judge whether one way is better than another, or are they all equally good options? Ought we to inculcate fidelity to a particular religion in our children, or should we simply teach them how to be intelligent consumers when they grow up and encounter the great marketplace of religions on their own?

Most people naturally gravitate to some position on these issues, which they instinctively feel to be right, and thus may not perceive a problem in deciding what to think about other religions. Education and actual encounters with other religious traditions and institutions can certainly help shape and refine attitudes and alleviate the perennial problems of misunderstanding. However, in my experience, other problems emerge, not when Christians actually encounter people of other faith traditions, but when Christians gather and talk among themselves about these issues, and find that their fellow churchgoers do not necessarily share their deeply held convictions about other faiths. Things can quickly break down when accusations of "betrayal of the gospel" or "intolerance and triumphalism" begin to fly, and when the discussants lack the concepts and language to talk about the historical, sociological, psychological, and theological underpinnings of their positions. As I have observed over many years of talking to congregations and teaching college students and seminarians about religious diversity, it is quite a hot, and potentially divisive, issue.

The plan of this book, therefore, is to explore a wide range of issues relating to religious diversity. We begin with historical and sociological considerations in the first chapter, exploring the parameters of the current situation and analyzing it in terms of social and historical processes. We see that the encounter of two religious groups follows certain patterns throughout history. We also analyze the dynamic of encounter in the tension that arises between our natural need to maintain a sense of stability, loyalty, and integrity, and our need to build bridges to those outside our boundaries in order to avert conflict and foster good relations. I present this as the tension between "integrity" and "openness."

Then, in the next three chapters, we trace the history of Christianity's many encounters with and responses to the presence of other religions through several stages. At its inception, Christianity lived in the remarkably diverse world of the late Roman Empire, and, prior to its triumph as the official state religion in the early fourth century, had to deal theologically with Manichaeism, mystery cults, the traditional Roman cults, and many others. The emperor Constantine's declaration of toleration in the early fourth century, and the establishment of Christianity later that century by Theodosius, quieted things for a while by eliminating many of the other faiths in public life. It was true that the entire world had not converted, but Christians could feel certain that everyone in the known world had been evangelized completely, and so those outside the faith could be seen as having made their choices, and no one had the excuse of ignorance.

This complacency was shattered by the discovery of the New World and its unevangelized people, and new theologies emerged to deal with the fate of peoples that had existed for over a millennium after Christ without ever hearing the gospel. The Protestant Reformation also sparked a new interest in resolving problems of "the other," prompting new theological formulations. The third chapter deals with this middle period.

The fourth chapter closes the historical section with an account of the new crisis of the late-nineteenth and early-twentieth centuries as the opening of Asia gave rise first to a new optimism and burst of missionary activity. Later, this optimism gave way to a new realism as the expected mass conversions failed to materialize and religious diversity began to appear to be permanent. This chapter recounts the history of the theologies that emerged in response to the changing historical situations, leading to the vigorous outpouring of theologies at the time of Vatican II and the establishment of the World Council of Churches.

The fifth chapter surveys theological positions that are current today, organizing them into the four broad categories of exclusivism, inclusivism, pluralism, and parallelism. After indicating what each of these basic positions entails, I appraise the strengths and weaknesses of each position.

The sixth chapter addresses a fundamental tension that arises as Christians continue to confront the new world of religious diversity: Do we respond by redoubling missionary efforts, or do we engage the other in dialogue? Mission and dialogue are generally taken to be mutually exclusive options: One may believe that others' religions are deficient and that they need to adopt one's own; or one may believe that others' religions are on a par with one's own and thus worth attending to. This seems to force believers to choose either proclamation or dialogue, but we shall see that there are other ways to manage that tension.

My goal is that by the end of the book, readers should have in

hand an enhanced understanding of the outlines of the problem of
diversity, a sense of the history of the Church's dealings with it, and
a set of conceptual tools for thinking through the problems on their
own, in parish education settings, or informal discussion groups.
This book is therefore principally a guide for navigating the ways of
thinking about religious diversity in order to facilitate more informed discernment. It is not written to provide readers with ready-
made answers.

There are two other approaches to religious diversity that we
will *not* be examining in these pages. The first is the nonreligious approach, which brackets out actual religious beliefs and the concerns
of religious communities in order to consider the problem of diversity from a strictly social-scientific or historical approach. The other
is the approach of the increasing number of people who describe
themselves as "spiritual but not religious" and who tend to see religious belief purely as a matter of personal discretion. Their approach
minimizes the more problematic aspects of religious diversity by dis-
regarding the communal lives of religious people and reducing all
religion to a free individual choice not subject to comment or critique from others. We will exclude the nonreligious and individual-
istic perspectives from our considerations. Our primary audience is
understood to be people who belong to organized Christian Church
bodies, and who are striving to understand how they, as individuals
in faith communities, can conduct informed discussions and come
to an agreement on the meaning and challenge of religious diversity.

I

Social and Historical Elements

In April 1992 Rodney King uttered a phrase that instantly entered the American psyche and became part of the common lexicon, as durable and recognizable as Nancy Reagan's "Just say no," or Sally Fields's "You like me! You really like me!" Earlier, the public airing of a videotape showing Los Angeles police officers beating him had led to the trial of those officers on charges of excessive force. When they were acquitted, riots broke out in Los Angeles that lasted three days, and during the chaos, a television news crew interviewed King to get his reaction. With a look of great pain on his face, he said, "Can't we all just get along?"

Conflict is real, and it is painful. As we look at the modern world—where Protestants and Catholics battle in Northern Ireland, a thirty-year war between Sinhalese Buddhists and Tamil Hindus is only just beginning to abate in Sri Lanka, and Western analysts talk about "Islam's bloody borders"—it seems to people of goodwill everywhere that much could be solved if those who are in conflict would just sit down and talk. "Getting along," it seems, should be a simple matter of discipline and will: Give up all intention of violence, and it will go away. It should be easy, and the benefits are obvious.

So why does it not happen?

To ask this question about religious conflicts is to assume that religions in all times and places function as they do at present in the United States, where the government largely leaves religious groups to their own devices and where no religion has sufficient power or authority to exercise coercion over any other. Religions can get together and dialogue because of specific social and historical conditions that make dialogue possible. Such conditions are present in contemporary U.S. society, but this is a recent and hard-won development.

Furthermore, to ask this question assumes that religions primarily set out beliefs and doctrines among which individuals can pick and choose and about which groups can differ. The reality is that religions are much more than this. They perform other functions than simply providing a way of looking at the world that is personally satisfying for individuals. Their rituals provide ways for communities to come together and build an identity; they serve as symbols for a group's aspirations; in some places they serve as the basis for the ways in which civil society is structured and functions. Factors such as these make religions' beliefs and practices far less negotiable than many Americans can realize.

In this section we will examine a few key sociological principles and historical developments that influence the tone and direction of interreligious relationships. Without this background the theological reflections that constitute Part Two will be speculative and abstract, unmoored in the actual conditions of human society and history.

1
Sociological and Theoretical Considerations

Religion

One of the difficulties that we have when we talk about "religious diversity" arises from the vocabulary itself. Though both *religion* and *diversity* are common words that we use every day, the word *religion* poses special problems when we put it into historical and sociological perspective. (The word *diversity* has its own difficulties, as we shall see by the end of this chapter.) In the first place, the word *religion* has meant different things in different periods of western history. In the second place, many of the "religions" with whom we seek dialogue lack, or have only recently acquired under western influence, a word that corresponds to our word *religion*. Those difficulties are too broad and complex to tackle here, but one task we should attend to at the outset is to make clear what *we* are going to mean by the word *religion*.

That is important, because the way we understand this word will influence the way we handle questions of religious diversity. If we are going to deal with the questions that arise because of the presence of many religions on the scene, then we need to be able to distinguish those religions from other cultural and social phenomena that we find there as well: political, ideological, artistic, and so on. We can eliminate those from the discussion right away because we cannot see them as part of the same logical class as Christianity.

Political parties and sports leagues, while performing some of the same functions and eliciting the same level of emotion and commitment as religions, clearly operate within different spheres and do not compete with Christianity (one may be a member of the Republican Party and a Chicago Cubs fan without feeling that either conflicts with one's being a Christian).

Some things, however, are not so easy to dismiss. It has been suggested, for example, that Marxism ought to be classed as a religion because, in many respects, it resembles one in its beliefs and functions, and it seems harder to square being a Marxist with being a Christian (although it has been done). Does this mean that when considering the relationship of Christianity with other religions such as Buddhism, Judaism, and Hinduism, we must also consider its relationships with Marxism? with existentialism? with atheism? Do these count as elements within the phenomenon of religious diversity? One way to handle these questions is to present a definition of religion, for that will give us a paradigm to guide our thought. Let us adopt the following definition as a way of clarifying the issues we will be discussing throughout this book:

> Religion is that frame of mind that sees both meaning and motivations for action as coming from the world outside the human realm, as well as all the practices and institutions to which this frame of mind gives rise.

This definition opposes "religion" to "humanism," which I take to mean a frame of mind that derives meaning and motives strictly from within the human realm. An example of a humanistic institution would be the U.S. Supreme Court, which devotes itself to the interpretation of texts (the Constitution and Bill of Rights) with all the zeal of a Christian biblical scholar. Nevertheless, none of the court's justices believes that these documents were either revealed by God or discovered by an enlightened human being as part of the fabric of reality. Rather, they acknowledge the texts to be human products, plain and simple. Human beings composed them, and human interpretation keeps them meaningful.

Religion, on the other hand, derives its view of the world, its analysis of the human situation, and its recommendations for human ethics and action from reality itself, denying that what it sees are nothing more than human inventions. Whether revealed by God or a set of gods, or retrieved from the empyrean realm by great seers and sages, religion finds its meaning and motives in reality itself and demands that human beings conform their own lives, beliefs, and actions to this reality. Religion "breaks in," or is "brought in," from outside the human realm and commands assent; humanism believes that human beings create meanings and motivations for themselves, and demands that human beings therefore take responsibility for their own inventions.

This means that *religious* diversity refers strictly to the diversity of ways in which human beings look to reality itself to find truth, values, and motives. Marxism, by this measure, is a humanistic phenomenon, denying that real meaning and ethics can be retrieved from or discovered in the nature of things themselves and demanding that human beings create their own system of economic and social structures as best they can. As such, it might compete for allegiance and assent with *all* religions, and present itself as an alternative to the religious worldview, but it would not be part of the diverse community of religions itself. The systems of thought and practice that we will be dealing with in this book, therefore, will be those that together compete to be the real alternative to all humanistic systems. Christianity shares this competition with Buddhism, Hinduism, Islam, and others, but not with existentialism or Marxism.[1]

It is also important to realize that this definition of religion implies the existence of *religions*, in the plural. That is, we can define *religion* only by abstracting it as a concept from concrete "religions," frames of mind that real people maintain that affirm some actual picture of reality. Whether it is a picture of a humanity alienated from God by original sin to be redeemed through Jesus Christ, or of a humanity endlessly wheeling around in a meaningless merry-go-round of birth-death-rebirth that requires a means of liberation, to be religious means to affirm some fairly specific picture of reality that gives rise to a particular set of meanings and motivations. This in turn requires an affirmation that such a concrete position is possible. The point may seem obvious, but I raise it here to indicate that the set of elements comprising religious diversity excludes not only humanistic positions (which take particular stands against religion) but also the nonposition of agnosticism. The denial that humanity ever could marshal the resources necessary to affirm any particular view of reality, while it is a position of sorts, is not a religious position, and falls outside the discussion of religious diversity.[2]

Thus, by applying this definition of religion, we focus our attention on a community of competing systems that claim to see both meaning for life and motivation for action as inscribed in reality itself and denies that these have to be invented by humans and for humans. We are excluding from this community systems that either deny such externally existent truths or deny the capability of humans to settle the question one way or the other. If all such views were taken together, we might speak of a comprehensive diversity of human views of meaning and purpose, but in this book, we will be talking strictly of *religious* diversity, and so we leave the latter two types of position, the humanistic and the agnostic, out of the discussion.

I hope this definition also makes clear that religion has both personal and social dimensions. In the past, the word *religion* referred primarily to its public aspects, its buildings and its rituals.[3] During the nineteenth century, as more nations in Europe and the Americas separated religion and the state, religion retreated to the private sphere, with the result that people came to regard it more and more as a matter of personal preference and choice. It was only at this time that the word *faith* became synonymous with the word *religion*. I want to be sure that in this book we realize that religion encompasses both the individual and the social group, because issues of religious diversity do not arise only between individual people, but between the aggregates that we call "Buddhists" or "Christians." The bonds that keep these groups together, and the way in which the presence of other groups affects those bonds, must be part of our study. We must balance issues of both personal conscience and institutional life in all our considerations.

Sociological Observations

When we talk about religious diversity in contemporary America, we need to understand it as a very particular and historically peculiar phenomenon. It has frequently been observed that the United States (as well as Europe and other places) represents something very much like a "marketplace of religions."[4] This phrase depicts the current situation as one in which many different religions coexist as competitors in a free market. None of them can compel or coerce the allegiance of its members because none has the backing of the political or military authorities to enforce loyalty and obedience, and none commands such overwhelming numbers or power that it can exert pressure on members of other religions to "switch brands." In such a setting, religions have no other recourse than literally to *market* themselves in an effort to attract adherents, whose membership, therefore, results from the free choice they make as "consumers."

Many people recognize the benefit of belonging to a religion of some kind, and because of that they are "in the market." However, the actual choice they make between one religion and another will subject them to only a minimal risk of social repercussions. As long as they choose a religion whose teachings and practices predispose people to contribute to society and discourage them from disturbing the peace, it will do. One may equally well choose no religion at all, as is done both by nonreligious people and those who describe themselves these days as "spiritual but not religious." Others may disapprove of the choice, and assert that people should join *their* group in preference to all others, but it is highly unlikely that one will have to endure any substantial social opprobrium or disability or any political or criminal reprisals on account of it. Unless the group is extravagantly exotic or obviously antisocial, one may choose one's religion without fear of being thrown in the lion's den or the fiery furnace. A phrase common in my youth, "Attend the church of your choice," can make sense only in such a setting. Interreligious dialogue and ecumenical activity are ways of ensuring domestic tranquility and promoting public virtue insofar as they keep the competition civil and foster cooperation (but not cartelization). We can even "celebrate diversity" as something good and enriching.

However, this open marketplace is something of an anomaly when seen in the sweep of global human history. If we look at the religious lives of tribal peoples, we see little evidence that they conceive of "religion" as anything separate from other aspects of the common life. The rituals enacted to mark seasons or life-cycle events and the stories told about gods and ancestral spirits dovetail into and provide support for all other features of social and economic life: family structures and responsibilities, inheritance customs, distribution of goods, hunting and farming practices, healing of illnesses—the list goes on. When religious concepts and practices pervade all aspects of social life in this way, it is little wonder that one does not see evidence of religious diversity or indeed any consciousness of "religion" as a category that comprises a whole class of "things" that can be lined up and examined with a consumer's eye. There is only that which is taught and lived within the group.

Even after the growth of urban civilizations, one does not necessarily see the arising of religion as such. Trevor Ling, in a study of the life of the Buddha, published in the 1970s, makes the observation that what we think of today as the great religions—Buddhism, Judaism, Islam, Christianity, Confucianism, and Hinduism—were once complete civilizations, setting the beliefs and practices of entire nations and empires.[5] The laws contained in texts such as the *Laws of Manu*, the Torah, and the Qur'an do not merely state a set of beliefs and prescribe a set of rituals. They contain complete codes of civil and criminal law as well, setting the penalties for murder, regulating marriage and divorce, prescribing inheritance laws, and so on. They undergirded the social formation of the ancient nation of Israel and the great Islamic empires—Ummayad, Abbasid, and Ottoman—that flourished for 1,300 years. They still play this role in many contemporary countries.

Confucianism likewise prescribed the role of the emperor and the proper duties of his ministers. Until the arrival of Buddhism in China around the time of Christ, it saw its competition arising not from other "religions" (a concept that did not exist), but from rival political schemes, primarily legalism and Mohism (which were themselves mixtures of things we would regard as religious and political). Hinduism, a composite religion that made room for a wide variety of cults and deities within a single, flexible conceptual umbrella, likewise included texts such as the *Laws of Manu* that, from an early period, prescribed social forms and legal institutions based on religious legitimations. These religions contained words (*dharma* in Sanskrit and *li* in Chinese) that connoted both the orderly working of nature and the principles underlying human morality and duties, making a single world order that combined both the social and the natural. Both believed that when human relations were properly ordered and everyone performed the duties attending their place in society, the natural world would also be in order and there would be no plagues, droughts, hailstorms, or other disasters.

Perhaps most significant for readers of this book, it is well to remember that before the Protestant Reformation and the subsequent Age of Enlightenment (the sixteenth to eighteenth centuries), *Christianity* was actually *Christendom*, a large geographic area where Christianity prevailed, providing the underpinning for social and legal practice (as in the blessing of marriages and the proscription of usury) and legitimating the political order (as when the bishop crowned the new king). Our current understanding of Christianity as a system of beliefs and practices from which an individual may freely choose among a menu of "religions" with no effect on either natural phenomena or the smooth functioning of society, and indeed with no particular price to be paid for the choice beyond the fate of the individual soul, is a vastly different way of seeing religion's scope and role.[6]

When a religion provides the rationale and legitimation for an entire civilization, then religious diversity does not appear as a positive good to be "celebrated." Rather, the appearance on the scene of an alternative set of beliefs, scriptures, rituals, and law codes represents a dire threat. Rather than being good in the sense that it puts more products on the market, thus giving consumers a wider choice, it appears more like sedition. Imagine someone recommending that the United States scrap the Constitution and the Bill of Rights in favor of a whole new set of civil laws and political structures, and the picture becomes clear.

But the traditional function of religion goes beyond providing for a set of laws and social structures that help hold nations together. Several theorists such as Peter Berger and Roy Wagner have pointed to a much more profound and pervasive function of religion: that of building entire worlds. They point out that the world does not immediately make sense to the human mind. All that our senses give us of the world is a raw, unprocessed jumble of shapes and colors, sounds, smells, tastes, and other sensations. It is up to the mind to take all this information and arrange it into meaningful patterns. When that does not happen, then we are like the protagonist of C. S. Lewis's novel *Out of the Silent Planet,* a man named Ransom, who is kidnapped and taken to Mars. When he first emerges from his spaceship and looks at the Martian landscape, he is panicked—he cannot make out anything; it is a riot of colors and shapes that do not resolve into anything intelligible. He has to learn, with the help of others, what everything is and how each thing relates to other things.

As individuals, we cannot accomplish this feat on our own. Instead, a whole picture of "the way things are" (a total image that Berger calls the *nomos,* or the "order of things") is largely given to us by our parents, teachers, friends, and others within our society. We learn that the patch of green and brown before us is a "tree," and we learn what trees are "for" and what they "mean." But more than this, we learn about other people, and we learn about the hidden structures behind things. We learn, for example, that the king is enthroned because the creator of the world, God, consecrated him and his lineage for that role. Or perhaps we learn that all people are equal because God created them equal, meaning that no one is privileged to rule simply by virtue of their birth.

In the premodern societies described above, where one religion predominates, children will be educated by all the social institutions within which they grow (the family, the school, the local temple, etc.) to see the world in that religion's terms. That particular worldview, if it is taught thoroughly and if there are no competing visions on the scene, will take hold as the plain, commonsense view of "the way things are." Anything that chips away at the plausibility of this world-view will thus be extremely threatening. Again, it will not be perceived as a welcome addition to the range of choices available; rather, it will bring with it a threat of chaos, inducing the very panic that Ransom felt when he found himself unable to visually interpret the landscape of Mars. This is a far deeper threat than political chaos; this portends a breakdown of reality itself, bringing with it confusion and even madness.

It is no wonder, then, that historically most languages have lacked a word that corresponds strictly to *religion* as we use it today, to indicate a class of belief systems that all seek meaning and motivations for action from outside the purely human realm; that are primarily directed at the comfort, salvation, or enlightenment of individuals; and that can easily coexist within a single given society. When one religion undergirds the entire social, legal, economic, and familial institutions of society, and when it provides a comprehensive framework for making sense of the world, then it is not just one religion among others, it is "the way things are," pure and simple. It is only with the advent of the modern world, in the historical moment when many of these worldviews have discovered how to account for the others in such a way that they can abide together in peace, that we can think about religious diversity as something good.

Let us take a brief look at processes that have ensued many times throughout history as religions have encountered each other prior to this moment.

Processes and Outcomes of Encounter

After the fall of the Roman Empire, European society lost its political cohesion and fell into a number of nations. Its Christian religious consensus remained intact, however, and spread even farther into northern Europe, thanks to the efforts of missionaries. Thus, Christendom came into being, and even if England and Germany had their own kings, those kings were sanctioned by and understood their roles in terms of Christian teachings. Europeans were certainly aware of groups of non-Christians: the Jews in their midst, the "heretics" that appeared from time to time to present novel teachings, later the Muslims off the eastern borders, and the vast number of polytheists or idolaters that had once populated the Roman Empire and were still to be found south in Africa and east in Asia. In this context, the word *religion* meant Christianity, or sometimes in a more restricted sense, it meant life in a monastery or convent. All the other alternatives, being false, were simply not religions.

Any religious system that has achieved this kind of hegemony does not easily or willingly relinquish it. It took decades of warfare and contention before Protestantism proved it was not just another heresy but was in Europe to stay. In China, Confucianism tried to counteract the appeal of Buddhism for many centuries after its arrival, especially when Buddhist monks claimed exemption from taxation, forced labor, military service, and the obligation to bow to their parents and emperor. To this day powerful movements are present in India to make it an exclusively Hindu state and to restrict or suppress Islam and Christianity. In all these cases, the dominant religion, with state backing, tried to deal with other religions in three ways: elimination, containment, and expulsion.

Elimination can mean either the literal eradication of all followers of a rival religion, or it can mean simply eliminating the religion itself by converting its followers to the dominant faith. Typically, medieval Christendom dealt with both Jews and heretics in both these ways. In extreme cases, movements arose in various places to exterminate the followers of other faiths, like the execution of individual leaders of heretical movements or the wholesale slaughter of Jews that took place from time to time, such as during the episode of plague known as the Black Death of 1348–49. More commonly, pressure was applied to members of dissident religions to convert to the dominant faith. When, for example, the last Muslim rulers were expelled from Spain in 1492, the Jewish community was given a choice either to leave or to convert. The Spanish Inquisition was set up originally to examine the newly adopted Christian faith of these *conversos* and ensure that it was sincere; the inquisitors did not want to find that the newly converted were professing Christianity publicly but practicing Jewish rituals in secret. Whether by the sword or by conversion, the strategy of elimination seeks to eradicate all alternative religions from society's midst.

Containment does not seek the abolition of other religions, but instead tries to confine them to certain quarters in order to insulate the wider society from their influence; it is rather like quarantining someone with a contagious disease to protect the public. The clearest example of this strategy from European history is the confinement of Jews to ghettos, but it has been used in other places and times as well. For instance, in Ming dynasty China (1348–1644), the emperors allowed Christian missionaries from Europe to enter, but strictly controlled their places of residence and their movements. In modern Saudi Arabia, foreigners live in walled compounds to keep them separate from the general population, and the government tightly controls the practice of non-Muslim religions.

Expulsion refers to either sending followers of other religions out of a territory seen as "belonging" to one religious group, or mounting defenses to keep other religions from entering in the first place. As mentioned above, those Jews who did not convert to Christianity after 1492 were sent out of Spain. At the same time, Islam was seen mostly as an external threat by Western European Christian authorities, and so a great deal of effort was expended to maintain the borders and keep that threat out. In a very real sense, the partition of India and the creation of Pakistan in 1947 was a mutual expulsion meant to separate two religions to their own territories.

All three strategies—elimination, containment, and expulsion—form the primary historical means by which a given religion deals with its rivals when it is in a position to do so. As should be clear by now, the motivation behind these strategies comes with the threat of impending chaos that the alternatives represent. It is simplistic to view them as nothing more than the means deployed by a privileged elite to maintain their dominance. Even the relatively powerless peasant or foot soldier, having grown up under a certain system and having been educated to a certain worldview, will look at the appearance of other religions as something to be feared, and averted if possible. It is only when the existing order has already shown itself to be inadequate and some new alternative presents a chance to reestablish order that new religious movements will be welcomed in. For example, Rodney Stark has demonstrated that traditional Roman religion was literally killing the empire when Constantine, seeing an opportunity to replace it with something much more functional, legalized Christianity and called off the persecutions.[7] Likewise, centuries later, the Roman Empire was moribund and its political structures in North Africa had become largely ineffective, making for great corruption and confusion in local government. Islam, preceded by a reputation for fairness and good government, swept across the Mediterranean coast because it presented the population with a welcome opportunity to restore order and improve people's lives. But in situations where a political and social order is already in place, new arrivals will not be welcomed; they will be resisted as threats to the order. Unless one understands the deep-seated fear of chaos, one will not be able to grasp why earlier societies did not embrace diversity as a positive.

In the next three chapters, we will examine the religious history of Western Christianity to see how we moved from viewing diversity as a threat to seeing it as something to celebrate. Before turning to that subject, we must examine one last theoretical element that has more to do with individual and group psychology than with history: the tension between openness and integrity.

Openness and Integrity: Balance and Tension

One may get the impression from what has been said so far that premodern societies are monolithic, with all their members in perfect lockstep and harmony. In fact, sociologists point out that even the most solidly entrenched social system is far from uniform. Conditions change, old explanations no longer work, people simply differ from one another in outlook and temperament. Even when Europe was Christendom and was attempting to minimize the threat of other religions by the three strategies outlined above, those strategies were never wholly successful; lines of communication still existed, and ideas did flow back and forth. Given that there is always awareness of alternatives to one's own or one's group's beliefs and practices, how do we deal with this? When do we resist, and when do we accommodate? I propose that throughout our history, we have had to strike a balance between two opposing tendencies that I will call "openness" and "integrity." By looking at this process, we will come to understand that, even today, a person's or a society's religion is not simply a matter of intellectual choice, where one weighs the alternatives and then chooses freely. Instead, it involves a dynamic interplay of social forces whose contents and consequences we may not even be able to articulate.

We are fundamentally social beings. Except for the few who leave human society and are never heard from again, even the most solitary among us is part of a social structure and lives in relationship with others. Our basic impulse is to form groups, and thus we want to build bridges to others. On the other hand, to be part of a social group is, as we have seen, to be educated in its worldview and morals, and to feel threatened by anything that undermines these. This fear imposes limits on how far we can go to accommodate ourselves to another's point of view or lifestyle. The first tendency is what I am calling "openness," because it leads us to be open to others and meet them halfway in order to connect with them; the second I am calling "integrity" because through it we maintain a sense of who we are and what the world is like. I am not saying that we must choose between these two modes of relating to others. Instead, they form the two ends of a continuum, and we find ourselves in various situations somewhere in between them, seeking to make connections with others while at the same time maintaining our own limits and boundaries.

Clinging to either extreme is neither healthy nor desirable. If one moves too far to the openness end of the spectrum, then one will be too accommodating, saying yes to everyone about everything, even when it embroils one in contradictions. If a person is so driven to connect with others that she or he will agree to everything, then at some point others will begin to wonder if such a person has any moral center at all, or any kind of consistent core identity. As the contradictions pile up, others will learn not to trust that individual, because the yes given to everything becomes meaningless.

On the other hand, a person who moves too far to the integrity pole will tend to see every issue, no matter how trivial, as one on which to take a stand and man the barricades. Sociologists and social psychologists have long noted how, in a political arena marked by multiple political parties, one generally finds two or three large parties in the center flanked by smaller parties that diminish in size as their views become more narrowly ideological. The Republican and Democratic parties dominate the U.S. scene because they are "big umbrellas" that can accommodate a wide variety of views on individual topics without falling apart. Smaller fringe parties at both the conservative and liberal ends remain small because they cannot unite; the smallest disagreement entails a break because of the overwhelming instinct to preserve a total integrity that permits no compromise. One is reminded of Garrison Keillor's tale of the Sanctified Brethren, a group with only sixteen members that splits over the issue of whether to offer water to a non-Christian stranger; the "cup of cold water debate" divides them into two sects of eight members each.

Lest this humorous example trivialize the issue, let me emphasize that maintaining some kind of integrity is important both for the individual's psychological well-being and for the maintenance of a stable social group. The boundary between openness and integrity is guarded more by the heart and gut than by the head, and we know when the boundary has been reached because we feel a discomfort with those we encounter and the views they profess, as if accepting their point of view or their practices would amount to giving up ourselves. I can enter into dialogue with Buddhists, for example, because generally engaging in dialogue does not threaten my own sense of self. I cannot, on the other hand, even contemplate entering into dialogue with White Supremacist religious groups such as Christian Identity cells, because even to engage in dialogue implies a kind of legitimacy to their point of view that I cannot grant without feeling that I am betraying my deepest core values. I can only oppose them.

Almost no person or group of people takes their stand all the way at one end or the other of this spectrum. Most will find a point in between where the twin forces of openness and integrity come to a balance. In any encounter situation, the desire to build a relationship will be balanced by the awareness that one can only go so far in this endeavor before the disquieting feeling arises that one is giving away too much and infringing on one's integrity. This boundary will have to be discovered anew for every new person or group met and every new issue considered. In the area of interreligious relations, this tension will determine whether to engage in dialogue at all (where one can be open) and where one will engage in evangelism instead (where the other proves too unacceptable and dialogue would seem like betrayal of the self or the group). If one chooses the path of dialogue, this tension will also influence how one picks dialogue partners and what will be put on the table in dialogue.

We tend uncritically to associate the quality of openness with more liberal religious positions, and integrity with more conservative or fundamentalist theologies, but that is a mistaken association. Almost everyone has a sense of who they are and a set of core values. Along with these comes the possibility, even the likelihood, that one will encounter others who threaten this integrity with opposing and unacceptable opinions and practices. Sometimes I tell my students that if they examine themselves, they will find they are all fundamentalists *about something*. That is, they all have deeply rooted values that define who they are, and they all find themselves on occasion encountering views they cannot engage but must simply oppose. The liberal view, which values tolerance and celebrates diversity, will have trouble dialoguing with a religion of intolerance that seeks to eliminate or convert others. Once we know about the tension between openness and integrity, we can examine ourselves to find what constitutes our own integrity. This allows us to understand why we all inevitably find certain people or groups suitable for dialogue while avoiding or attempting to evangelize others.

The Parameters of Diversity

So far we have seen several things. First, we now know that politics and the presence of power have a great impact on how religions relate to one another throughout history. If one side or the other has coercive power on its side within a given geographic area, it will strive to maintain its position through elimination, containment, and expulsion, resorting to dialogue when it no longer has the ability to succeed with those strategies. When religions do come face to face in situations where genuine dialogue is possible, the dialogue will then proceed or not depending on the ability of individual groups or participants to negotiate the tension between integrity and openness. That is to say, when each side feels it can engage in dialogue in order to create community without staking too much of their own integrity in the process, then dialogue will go forward; otherwise, they will relate in other ways—mutual ignorance, border skirmishes, purely formal diplomacy with no real warmth, mutual proselytism, and so on.

One final nuancing of the picture remains to be done, however. Everything we have said so far is consonant with a picture of religious diversity as an issue between great communities. Typically in dealing sociologically with religious diversity or theologically with interfaith issues, the assumption is that we are talking about Buddhist-Christian or Muslim-Jewish relationships, where the primary "actors" are the religious traditions themselves. In reality, things are not so clearly defined. In my own work in interreligious dialogue, I have always been acutely aware that I was participating with a very particular (usually self-selected) group of fellow Christians in an encounter with a similarly particular (also usually self-selected) delegation from the other tradition. Whether I was at the International Buddhist-Christian Theological Encounters or at the conference Islam and the Dialogue of Civilizations, I knew that each side, Buddhist and Christian, or Muslim and Christian, also contained a sizable contingent of people who could not participate in the dialogues, whose sense of integrity dominated the need for openness. In short, neither my side nor the other side represented a total tradition engaged in dialogue.

The reason for this is that diversity is not a phenomenon to be observed only between religious traditions. If any tradition consists of both those who do and those do not wish to meet in dialogue, it is because traditions themselves embody diversity. Furthermore, the same dynamic of openness versus integrity also operates at this level. Within Christianity, for example, ecumenical meetings are aimed at effecting greater unity within the Body of Christ. Some Christians, wishing openness, will come to the table for these dialogues; others, wishing to maintain a denominational integrity, reject them as dangerous. Then again, within denominations and ecclesial communities themselves, issues arise that divide people (the current debates over homosexuality and same-sex unions within many Christian denominations are a good example). Whether dialogue can take place across those divides is again a function of the tension between openness, the wish to maintain communion, and a drive to integrity, which causes a breach of that communion as one side or the other finds that it can no longer even meet the other for talks without excessive compromise. I have sometimes said that, if you trace this down, you can find diversity even between two people in the same pew in the same parish on a Sunday morning. The tension between openness and integrity affects life even at this level as parishes wrestle with controversies and try to adjudicate conflicting positions.

Thus, to understand religious diversity properly, we must come to understand that it is not merely a matter of noticing a number of "great religions," such as Hinduism, Islam, Christianity, Buddhism, Judaism, and others, that must somehow learn to manage their differences. Diversity can be noted *at all levels* of human community: the religion, the denomination, the local congregation, right down to the individual. Like the graphic mapping of a Mandelbrot set, the picture remains consistently complex no matter the level of magnification. This means that what will be said about religious diversity in the pages of this book could, to some extent and with the appropriate adjustments, be said about any two religious groups that confront each other over any issue at all, and probably also with regard to political groups, social classes, and other alignments of human beings at any level.

Conclusion

We have seen several things in this chapter. First, we are aware now that religion is closely linked to societies, and that the present situation of the "marketplace of religions," wherein different religious groups can enter into dialogue, is a recent development. Second, we have seen that in the past, religions provided a basis for social structures and practices in a more total way than they do in Western societies today, making incursions by alternative religions more of a threat than they are today. In consequence, most societies in the past dealt with them by the strategies of elimination, containment, or expulsion if they had the power. Third, we have seen that, both in the past and today, people and groups who encounter each other must negotiate the tension between openness and integrity, the urge to forge links with others and the need to maintain a stable set of values and identities. Finally, we have seen that diversity is a condition that pervades religious communities at all levels, making the concepts presented in this book applicable to encounters between traditions in their entireties or between smaller subgroups within them, even to the level of encounters between individuals.

Those are the sociological elements that go into interreligious encounter. A purely theological account of religious diversity, one that starts from first principles and ignores the realities on the ground, will fail to connect with the lives of people who live in societies, in history, and with often unspoken needs. Such a pure theology will not help people understand or come to terms with the issues of religious diversity.

For the next three chapters, we will go past these theoretical principles and turn to the concrete historical situation of European and North American Christianity to see how the Church has dealt with diversity in the past, and how our present situation came into being.

2
Christianity and Other Religions in the Early Period

The previous chapter considered the historical and sociological processes of interreligious encounter in very broad theoretical terms; the next three chapters will focus on concrete historical events. We will begin by looking at the specific ways the Church and significant Christian thinkers have responded to the encounter with other religions through different historical periods. The previous chapter has, I hope, laid out a conceptual framework that will help us understand why this history took the particular trajectory it did, and when our historical narrative is finished, we will be in a position to see our present situation and the shape of contemporary theological responses to religious diversity within the twin contexts of sociological theory and our own religious history.

The Early Church in the Hellenistic World: A Historical Overview

Christians did not wake up one morning to find themselves suddenly faced with a motley religious landscape that was absent the night before. On the contrary, Christianity was born into a world of breathtaking religious variety, and from its beginning has had to face the challenges that diversity poses. In this section we will trace the development of this diversity from pre–New Testament times to the late Roman period, so that as we look at the New Testament and the writings of some early Church thinkers further on, we will be able to place them within their proper context.

Even before the birth of Jesus, Palestine had seen a remarkable rise in both religious and ethnic diversity, which had been building for centuries. After the return of the Jews from the Babylonian exile in 538 BC, Israel was a province of the Persian Empire and thus constantly interacting with its culture. As Alexander the Great and his army of Macedonian Greeks marched across Israel on their way to India in the late fourth century BC, they took over political control from the Persians and brought in a wave of Hellenistic culture. The Jews were able to shake off Greek rule in a revolt that lasted from 167 to 140 BC and enjoy a brief period of political autonomy, but in 63 BC the Romans conquered Palestine, and Roman soldiers and civilian administrators entered the land. The encounters between the Jews and the Persians, Greeks, and Romans were not always happy.

The Persian influence can be seen in the confrontations between two major rival groups of Judaism at this time: the Sadducees and the Pharisees. The former group, though somewhat open to interaction with Greek and later Roman culture, was religiously quite conservative. They accepted only the Torah (consisting of the Five Books of Moses) as scripture, and did not condone any innovation in belief and practice that could not be supported from it. The Pharisees, on the other hand, though less open to cultural interaction (their name, *perushim* in Hebrew, indicates "the separate ones"), were in fact more innovative in their beliefs. In addition to the Torah, they accepted the authority of other scriptures (such as the Psalms and the prophets), and, more important for our purposes, were more willing to incorporate beliefs imported from Persian religion into their theological framework.

Those beliefs will be familiar to Christian readers: the resurrection of the dead, a day of judgment, future rewards and punishments in the afterlife, and a belief in angels. That Jesus himself accepted these beliefs, and argued for them against the Sadducees, has led some scholars to believe that Jesus was a Pharisee, and that his disputes with the Pharisees in the Gospels reflect intra-Pharisaic debates over the interpretation and application of the law. We see, for instance, that it is Sadducees who tell the story of the woman who marries seven brothers after they die one by one, and then ask Jesus whose wife she will be in the afterlife; their purpose is to show how ridiculous they consider the idea of the resurrection of the dead to be. In his response defending resurrection, Jesus quoted only a verse from the Torah, because he knew his adversaries would not accept any other source as authoritative (Matt. 22:23–33). The notion of resurrection, as well as other religious ideas not found in earlier parts of the Old Testament, was already current before Jesus' time as a result of religious interactions with the Persians.

Greek religion had less direct influence because so much more of it plainly went against the grain of Jewish thought and practice than did Persian religion. After Alexander the Great defeated the Persian king Darius III in two battles in 333 and 330 BC, Palestine came under Greek control. The Ptolemaic and Seleucid Greek rulers[1] hoped the Jews would assimilate Greek culture to some degree, but Greek polytheism contradicted Jewish monotheism so starkly that a Jew was unlikely to participate in sacrifices to the Greek gods, and those few who did elicited tremendous disapproval. One Greek ruler in the centuries prior to the New Testament attempted to force Jewish participation in Greek rites, with disastrous results. In 167 BC, the ruler Antiochus IV Epiphanes issued an edict prohibiting the rituals and practices of traditional Judaism, set up a statue of Zeus in the Temple, and sacrificed a pig before it. He ordered all Jews to participate in the rites of Greek religion, including the sacrifice of unclean animals before Greek gods and ritual prostitution, and he sold the office of High Priest to the highest bidder. These actions provoked the family of the priest Mattathias and his sons to revolt, and for many years they carried on a guerrilla war against the Greeks, finally driving them out in 143 BC and establishing a semi-independent Jewish state for the first time since the Babylonian conquest four and a half centuries earlier.[2] This whole episode left the Jews unwilling to interact with foreign religions in a serious way thereafter. Although Greek religion may not have influenced Judaism all that much, Greek philosophy exerted a great attraction for many Jewish thinkers, and, as we shall shortly see, comprised a separate problem for Christian religious thought.

Religious interactions are never one-way, and Judaism had a great impact on Greek thought and culture. Beginning with the conquest of the northern kingdom of Israel in 722 BC and the southern kingdom of Judah in 587 BC, many Jews were forced into exile. In many cases they simply assimilated into their new cultural setting and thus were lost to Jewish history. However, in some places such as Babylon to the east and Alexandria to the west, they settled into communities together and maintained their practices and their identity. The Persian and Greek conquests established enormous empires covering vast territories under a single political regime, so travel became easier and more Jews migrated out of Palestine and settled in other localities. They thus became a leaven scattered throughout Greek culture.

During this period the Jews of the diaspora learned to speak Greek as their native language, and Hebrew, whose use was already declining in Palestine in favor of Aramaic, went out of use altogether in communities outside the territory of Israel. In the third century, according to the Jewish historian Josephus, the royal librarian at Alexandria, Egypt, approached the Greek king Ptolemy II Philadelphus (r. 283–246 BC), with a proposal to translate the Hebrew scriptures into Greek, and the king supported the project enthusiastically.[3] The result was called the *Septuagint*, after the Greek word for "seventy," because it was allegedly completed in seventy days by seventy scholars. In this way Jewish scriptures became accessible to a wider culture. Not only was it of use to Jews who could no longer speak or read Hebrew, but as the story of the royal sponsorship of the translation shows, non-Jews also had an interest in reading it. As Greek-Jewish interaction increased, many Greeks found themselves attracted to Jewish laws of hospitality and social justice, supported by the idea that there was only one God, before whom all were equal. However, even though rites existed for bringing outsiders into the Jewish community, most Greeks had no interest in adopting Judaism as a new ethnic identity, with the result that they remained on the threshold of the religious community, and appear in the New Testament as the "god-fearers" that were the friends and supporters of the Jews well into the first century AD.

Christianity emerged while Palestine was under Roman rule, a situation that was highly conducive to the appearance of multiple new religious movements. The Roman Empire spanned a broad arc of cultural and linguistic zones through which it inherited many pre-existing religions, including Judaism. In addition, as sociologist Rodney Stark points out, the early centuries of the Church's life were part of a period of intense religious ferment. In fact, it was this climate of earnest searching for new answers that enabled Christianity to enjoy the spectacular growth rates it did for its first two and a half centuries. As early as the time of Christ, traditional Roman religion had become highly dysfunctional. Its gods and goddesses did not care much about the fate of humanity, and its rituals and sacrifices existed in order to bribe them to intervene in human affairs, with no assurance that the divinities would not just take the bribes and still fail to act. Because the gods did not love anyone, belief in them gave people no reason to love each other, and so the empire limped as best it could from crisis to crisis with no social support networks to help people cope. For example, when plagues swept through, Roman religion provided no good reason for anyone to risk their lives by bringing food and water or providing basic nursing services to afflicted neighbors; this increased mortality rates. A cavalier attitude toward life gave rise to high rates of abortion and female infanticide; this lowered the rate of reproduction to below replacement levels. Consequently, the population was in decline, obliging the government to recruit a steady flow of immigrants to cultivate abandoned agricultural estates and repopulate cities, resulting in ethnic tensions and frequent communal riots in the urban areas. Consciously or unconsciously, the people knew that their traditional religion could not help them manage these crises, and they were open to new options.[4] Christianity's beliefs and practices made it the ideal candidate to provide a foundation for a more integrated and functional society, and people gravitated toward it, so that throughout this period it enjoyed a steady growth rate of 40 percent per decade.

But however much this religious openness benefited Christianity, it also created challenges. High demand for new religious options created a "religious marketplace," and other religions appeared on the scene, adding to the diversity—and the competition. The Mystery religions, which initiated followers in secret rituals based on Roman, Greek, and Egyptian agricultural rites and myths, appeared in every city as another alternative. Christianity's mother religion, Judaism, also had communities all over the eastern part of the empire, and, as the Gospels themselves report, Roman citizens attached themselves to it as proselytes or as "god-fearers." Other religions such as Mithraism and Manichaeism also made inroads, and Greek philosophical movements such as Stoicism, Epicureanism, and Cynicism gained adherents. Thus, the early Church had to make decisions, both practical and theological, about how best to respond to the continuing vitality of Judaism and to the variety of "pagan" cults crowding the marketplace. Because during this period Christians were still debating and formulating their beliefs and practices, their decisions regarding other religions became part of the deposit of faith.

By the time Jesus appeared at the turn of the millennium, Israel was already host to a mixture of Jewish, Persian, Greek, and Roman religious ideas and practices, all living in close proximity and interacting. With this historical situation in mind, we can now begin looking at what the New Testament and the early Church fathers had to say about other religions.

The Gospel Witness

Within the Gospels themselves, we must understand Jesus' own teaching regarding other religions in light of the occupation of Palestine by the Roman Empire. The independent Jewish state founded by Mattathias and his sons, the Hasmoneans, did not achieve political stability, as the lack of a clear heir from the royal Davidic line opened the way for anyone with military backing to claim the throne. In 63 BC the Roman general Pompey came to intervene in power struggles that had reached a stalemate, and claimed the territory for

Rome. The new Roman government installed Herod not long after as its puppet ruler, a king who persecuted the Pharisees because of their objections to his rule, their refusal to recognize him as a Jew (his mother was non-Jewish), and their insistence on separateness. Hundreds of Pharisees were killed in the early years of his reign, adding to the esteem in which the populace held them. Greek-speaking Hellenistic culture continued to thrive within and around Israel's territory, and Jews were faced with the task of deciding for themselves how much interaction with Hellenism was proper. Thus, as we read the Gospel accounts, we see Jesus constantly encountering non-Jews, both god-fearers living within Israel and those living outside its boundaries, during his travels through the Syro-Phoenician territories to the north. The stories of these encounters have been the primary sources of scriptural citation for Christian thinkers and writers trying to determine the proper response to other religions.

It appears from the stories of those encounters that Jesus was quite open to the possibility that God works for those outside the Jewish community. In the Gospel of Luke, Jesus' first public sermon after his return from the desert consists of a reading from the Book of Isaiah followed by his commentary, in the course of which he points out to the congregation that in two instances within the Old Testament, God brought comfort and healing to Gentiles rather than Israelites. The congregation gathered at the synagogue in Nazareth is so enraged by this that they attempt to throw him over a cliff (Luke 4:16–28). Later in his ministry, he puts those views into action by repeatedly giving his attention to outsiders: preaching to them, healing them, reviving their dead children, and commending their faith. At times he seems reluctant to help them, as when in Matthew 10:5–6 he sends the twelve apostles out on a mission and instructs them not to enter any Gentile territory or any Samaritan towns, but to preach "only to the lost sheep of the house of Israel," and when he initially refuses to grant the request of a Canaanite woman to cast a demon from her daughter, he again states, "I have been sent only to the lost sheep of the house of Israel" (Matt. 15:24). Nevertheless, in the end he seems to accept faith in him and in God wherever he finds it. The

Canaanite woman meets his refusal with an astute retort, and Jesus relents and grants her wish, exclaiming, "You are a woman of great faith!" (Matt. 15:28). In Matthew 8:10–11 he heals a centurion's son with similar praise for the man's faith, and adds a verse often cited by theologians who wish to argue for more openness in Christianity: "I assure you that many will come from the east and from the west and sit down with Abraham, Isaac, and Jacob at the feast in the kingdom of heaven" (Matt. 8:11; see also Luke 7:1–10).

Samaritans, traditionally enemies of the Jews, figure prominently in several episodes from the Gospels. In Luke 17:11–19 Jesus heals ten lepers, but the only one who returns to give him thanks is a Samaritan. In John, chapter four, Jesus preaches to a Samaritan woman, offering her the "living water" of God. He affirms that her community's worship on Mount Gerizim is not to be superseded by worship at the Temple in Jerusalem, nor does he insist that she and her fellow townsmen become proselytes to the Jewish community. When he tells the parable of the good Samaritan (Luke 10:29–37), he deliberately praises the Samaritan's helpfulness over the uncaring attitudes of the Levite and the priest, who allowed concerns for ritual purity to outweigh compassion for the injured traveler. To give one last example, in Matthew 25:31–44, as Jesus expounds the day of judgment in the parable of the sheep and the goats, he makes it clear that those judged are from "all the nations," and those who are judged righteous and allowed into the kingdom of heaven are not chosen solely from the Jewish people, nor are those who are condemned all Gentiles. The criterion of judgment is, as in the parable of the good Samaritan, the willingness to engage in acts of charity and compassion. Thus, when Jesus approves of and affirms those outside the Jewish nation, it is either because they have expressed faith in his ability to heal and revive or because he commends their acts of *agape.*

However much these and similar passages suggest an openness on the part of Jesus to finding God at work beyond the accepted boundaries, an openness that Christians might emulate, it must be counterbalanced by other verses and episodes that point to a more exclusionary attitude. Surely no verse is better known in this regard than the dictum of John 14:6: "I am the way, the truth, and the life; no one goes to the Father except by me." This image is reinforced in the following chapter when Jesus speaks of himself as the "true vine": "I am the vine, and you are the branches. Whoever remains in me, and I in him, will bear much fruit; for you can do nothing without me. Whoever does not remain in me is thrown out like a branch and dries up; such branches are gathered up and thrown into the fire, where they are burnt" (John 15:5–6). More conservative Christians who wish to argue against too much acceptance of other religions frequently cite these and related sayings of Jesus.

In the end, what are we to make of the Gospel witness? What *was* Jesus' teaching about the religions of the nations? Do the more open verses contradict the more closed ones? Does Jesus commend to his followers an attitude of acceptance or exclusion? Three observations may help resolve these tensions.

First, we must remember that the situation Jesus addresses in the Gospels is not our situation. There was no Christian Church at that time as a global, multiethnic group beyond the Jewish community, and by his own account, Jesus was sent to minister only to Israel and to preach the inbreaking of the kingdom of heaven. His vision for Israel is an eschatological vision that balances the "already" with the "not yet." The image of all nations gathered together in the world to come predates Jesus, and he uses it to illustrate the perfecting of the world only at the end of time. But Jesus also proclaimed that the kingdom was already being established, and his approval of *some* non-Jews must be seen as tokens in earnest that this vision will ultimately be fulfilled. The "not yet" aspect, however, precludes any assumption that all people in the present world are saved without exception.

Second, in no instance does Jesus ever commend the actual religion (whatever it may be) of those he encounters. He commends the Canaanite woman, the Samaritan leper, and the centurion for their faith *in him*. Never does he conclude his miracles by telling them it is all right to return to the worship of Apollo or the rural fertility goddesses. In other cases he commends non-Jews for demon-

2 Social and Historical Elements

strating in their actions the values of both Jewish religion and the
coming kingdom: hospitality, compassion, and placing more importance on human life than on ritual correctness. Again, this hardly
amounts to a blanket endorsement of other religions as such.

The above two points, taken together, show clearly that Jesus
approved of some outside the Jewish community because their attitudes and deeds reflected *his* teachings, not because they followed
other teachings that he deemed to be equally good. The third point
challenges the very terms in which we think of the problem. In our
modern situation, we are trying to discern what attitude Christians
should adopt toward other religions. We must realize that this is *not*
the problem with which Jesus grappled. If he displayed some hesi-
tation in his dealings with Samaritans, Greeks, Romans, and Syro-
Phoenicians, it was not because they practiced other religions, but
because they belonged to different, non-Jewish ethnic groups. Could
God, who was the God of the people of Israel, the descendants of
Abraham, work on behalf of unrelated peoples? When this point is
understood, then the tension between Jesus' recognition of real holiness in the lives of non-Jews and his declarations that he is the only
way to God eases considerably. He is affirming the Jewish *religion* as
he understands it, but grappling with the prospect that it might also
touch the lives of people of different *ethnicities*. As we shall see in the
next section, this particular question was not settled with a "yes"
until after Jesus' death and Resurrection, and only then did the question of the status of other *religions* arise.

Later New Testament Writings
The day of Pentecost is traditionally regarded as the "birthday of the
Church." However, it is well to remember that even at this crucial
time, there was no "Church," if by that we mean an institution entirely separate from Judaism with its own developed and articulated
beliefs and practices. As we have just seen, Jesus, as a rabbi and mes-
sianic figure ministering to the "lost sheep of the house of Israel,"
only confronted questions regarding the status of non-Jews vis-
à-vis the covenant between God and the *people* (not the *religion*) of

Israel. However, the issues facing the early Church were somewhat different. The Acts of the Apostles and the Epistles of the New Testament show us a new set of concerns as Christianity began to grow and take root in a world alive with many religions. In particular, these books had to articulate the relationship between a nascent Christian community and its parent people, the Jews, and the relationship of Christianity to a host of other, unrelated religions, whether long-entrenched or up-and-coming. We will begin by looking at New Testament passages that seek to answer the question of how Christians ought to relate to the Jews, a question that remains unique to this day in Christian thinking about interfaith relations. As we shall see in subsequent chapters, Christianity has always separated the problems of relations with Judaism from all others, since Judaism forms the matrix out of which Christianity sprang, and the Church always acknowledged that the Jews enjoyed a covenant with God that predated Christianity.

Early Christianity and Judaism. In the time immediately following Jesus' Resurrection and Ascension, Christianity was a small Jewish sect that proclaimed Jesus as the Messiah for whom all Jews had been waiting. They continued to follow the Jewish dietary laws, circumcise male children, and meet with the larger Jewish community in the synagogues. Thus, at first there was no real question about how to *relate to* the Jews; they *were* Jews. However, two factors helped to drive a wedge between the Christians and their mother community. First, the fact that Christians held Jesus to be the Messiah meant that they interpreted several passages of Jewish scripture differently from other Jews; it is for this reason that the Gospel of Matthew, thought to be directed primarily to a Jewish audience, places so much emphasis on the fulfillment of various scriptures in the life and ministry of Jesus. In effect, the Christians were stating that their opponents were not interpreting their own scriptures correctly, a contention that stimulated a great deal of scriptural study on the part of the dissenting Jews and contributed to the rise of the rabbinic traditions that assumed great importance in the formation of modern Judaism.

Second, as we have already seen, the monotheism and strong social and family ethic that pervaded Judaism were already attracting the attention of other citizens of the Roman Empire, leading many of them to either enter the Jewish community or ally themselves with it as god-fearers. Such people were also attracted to the Christian message for many of the same reasons: Christianity preached the one God who was the Father of all, which had the effect of binding strangers together in community and giving them a reason to care for one another. However, as Rodney Stark points out, both Judaism and primitive Christianity posed a barrier to their full participation. Judaism, it must be recalled, was not really a *religion* in the modern sense of the word; it was an *ethnicity*, and one does not convert to a new ethnic group. One might be adopted into it by various means, but one does not choose it as a "faith preference" while maintaining one's previous ethnic identity. Thus, both Judaism and early Christianity failed to make much headway in terms of solid growth.[5]

However, unlike Judaism at that time, Christianity adapted to this by rejecting the ethnic markers of Judaism, thereby dropping the barrier and opening a way for outsiders truly to convert. The crucial story is found in the tenth chapter of Acts, which recounts Peter's interactions with Cornelius, a god-fearer and regimental captain in the Roman army. Cornelius is described as a pious man and true friend of the Jewish community. One day, while he was at prayer, an angel appeared to him and told him to send for Simon Peter. At roughly the same time, Peter had a vision of a cloth descending from heaven filled with all kinds of animals while a voice instructed, "Get up, Peter; kill and eat!" (10:11–13). When Peter objected that he had never eaten anything unclean in his life, the voice reproved him, saying, "Do not consider anything unclean that God has declared clean!" (10:15). Immediately after the vision, Cornelius's messengers arrived and asked Peter to accompany them to Caesarea, and when he arrived at Cornelius's house and heard of the captain's vision, he exclaimed: "I now realize that it is true that God treats everyone on the same basis. Whoever worships him and does what is right is acceptable to him, *no matter what race he belongs to*" (10:34–35, italics added). This last phrase is telling, because it encapsulates the decisive point: Christianity was now to be considered a religion, not an ethnicity, and as such it was open to all regardless of their race. As the story continues, Cornelius and his household received the Holy Spirit and began speaking in tongues, after which Peter and his Jewish-Christian companions could not justify withholding baptism. The boundary that had existed between Cornelius and the Jewish community and relegated him to the status of god-fearer fell, and he was fully incorporated into the Christian community.

Afterward, when Peter returned to Jerusalem, he met with vigorous objections from the Jewish-Christian community there, which insisted that the new converts be circumcised and made to observe the dietary laws. After hearing reports of the parallel visions of Cornelius and Peter, however, they relented and decided not to impose those markers of Jewish identity, and by doing so, they opened the way for existing members freely to visit with and eat with Gentiles (Acts 11:1–18). The fact that the Christians had now fully accepted Gentile converts and had table fellowship with them aggravated the split between the Christians and the Jews, and Christians began to find that they were no longer welcome in some synagogues. With these developments in the first and early second centuries AD, Christianity developed a separate identity, and thus it begins to make sense to speak of Jewish-Christian relations. Contrary to much popular belief, however, relations between Jews and Christians remained cordial in many parts of the empire outside of Jerusalem well into the fourth and fifth centuries. Much of the anti-Jewish rhetoric that one finds in early Church fathers such as St. John Chrysostom has been attributed to their desire to break the bonds of friendship that many Christians continued to enjoy with Jews and to get the Christians under their care to stop attending synagogue services.

The apostle Paul was, if anything, more enthusiastic than Peter about ministering to the Gentile population, requiring no vision from God to go out and preach to anyone who would listen, and in Acts, chapter 18, we find him defending the conversion of Gentiles without their submission to the Jewish law before the Church in

Jerusalem, in terms similar to Peter's defense in Acts, chapter 11. Yet
even he was not insensitive to the significance of Christianity's Jewish heritage, and he struggled to understand how the covenant the
people of Israel had enjoyed related to the burgeoning and increasingly non-Jewish Christian Church. Some of his most sustained reflections on the question may be found in his Letter to the Romans.
In Romans, chapters 2 through 12, Paul embarks on a long consideration of the relationship between God, the Jews, and the Gentile
converts to Christianity, and throughout the letter, he is careful never
to derogate God's covenant with Israel or the status of the Torah,
which they received and kept. He is, however, convinced that the
Gentiles have been called through their faith in God every bit as
much as the Jews were called in the ancient past to be God's people.
But although the Gentiles can thus be saved through faith, Paul goes
on to say, in Romans 11:25–32, that eventually *all* the Jews will be
saved, because God's promise to them stands for all time.

These considerations, however, are peripheral to our main purpose. More to the point, we must be careful not to assume that Paul's
discussion centers on the question of how a bounded, self-contained
Christian Church is to relate to an equally bounded, self-contained
Judaism. He is trying to adjudicate differences between three different constituencies: Jews who have rejected the gospel of Jesus, Jews
who have believed in the gospel and constitute the Jewish branch of
Christianity, and Gentile converts and potential converts to Christianity who need to know whether or not they must become Jews in
order to be Christians, which would mean observing the dietary
laws, undergoing circumcision, and adopting a new ethnicity. Paul's
answer to this is no, but he tries to qualify his no in such a way that
he does not make the laws given in Jewish scripture unnecessary, or
God's covenant with the Jews null and void. Everything God has given
is good and lasting, so even though the Gentile converts must not
be required to submit to the terms of the Jewish covenant with God,
it does not follow that the covenant was given for nothing or that
being of the Jewish nation no longer counts for anything. Paul presents a vision in which the conversion of the Gentiles becomes part

of God's plan for eventually bringing all the Jews to salvation. Before that time, though, Paul needed to conceive a provisional framework that helps three overlapping, not distinct, communities relate to one another, and as we shall see in subsequent chapters, his framework still guides much Christian thought on relations with Jews.

The New Testament and the Gods of the Nations. If relating Judaism to Christianity presented a rather sticky problem to the New Testament writers, the matter of pagan religion was much more clear-cut. However, we must be careful in our reading of the evidence. Just as Jesus' conversations with and healings of various non-Jews have been interpreted as an open attitude toward the religions of the nations, so passages such as Acts 17:16–33, which records Paul's speech at the Areopagus on Mars Hill in Athens, have been taken as indicating that he too was willing to consider other religions as a pathway to God. In presenting the Christian case to the city councilors, Paul begins by noting that among the shrines to various deities that he has observed around the city, he found one with the inscription "To an unknown god." He goes on to identify this "unknown God" with the God of Israel who raised Jesus from the dead, and he even shows some familiarity with Greek philosophy and literature when he quotes the Platonic poet-philosopher Epimenides, "In Him we live and move and exist," and the Stoic poet Aratus, "We too are his children" (Acts 17:27). Could Paul have thought that the Greeks would worship God in pagan guise as an unknown god, and would he think that two pagan poets could have gained some kind of natural insight into God's nature and relationship with humanity?

Before deciding, let us look at other passages in which Paul refers to the pagan religions. The prelude to his discussion with the city councilors relates that, while walking around the city of Athens, Paul was "greatly upset" by the number of idols he encountered (Acts 17:16). In 1 Corinthians, chapter 8, Paul considers whether or not Christians may eat meat that has been offered to idols. Though he ultimately decides that it is not a good idea to eat such meat, which would have been distributed among worshipers after having been set as an offering before an image of a pagan deity, it is not because somehow the foreign god has contaminated it. Paul follows the line of the later Old Testament writings in declaring that the idols are mere statues that do not stand for anything, because besides God there are no other gods. Because other gods do not even exist, they cannot possibly contaminate or render impure the meat offered before them. Paul's relentless denigration of idol worship later caused a riot among the silversmiths of Ephesus, because they made a great part of their living fashioning idols of the goddess Artemis, and feared that Paul's teachings would ruin their business (Acts 19:21–41). In his first letter to the Corinthians, Paul refers to the pagan gods that the Corinthian Christians followed before their conversion as "lifeless idols" (12:2). In one instance Paul refers to idols as "demons" rather than as simple lifeless images (10:18–22). Taking all these passages together, one would be hard-pressed to interpret Paul's attitude toward idols and idol worship as anything other than negative.

Thus, while the speech in the Areopagus appears to leave some opening for valuing other religions as perhaps vehicles for God to speak to the pagans, in the overwhelming majority of cases, Paul is clearly against idol worship. His attitude appears to be driven by three concerns. First, he brings into Christianity the traditional Jewish belief that only God is worthy of worship; to worship anything other than God is an error. We see this concern clearly in one amusing episode in which, after Paul heals a man, the crowd in Lystra acclaims Paul as Zeus and Barnabas as Hermes and tries to worship them. Paul rebuffs this by stating that they are only men, and affirms that only God is entitled to be worshiped (Acts 14:8–18). This concern that only God be worshiped is repeated in a number of places in the New Testament (see also Gal. 4:8–11, Rev. 19:10, and Rev. 22:8–9).

Second, Paul, along with other New Testament authors, worries that members of the Christian Church are continuing to go to pagan temples, perhaps accompanying friends or family members. Paul points to the story of the Exodus as an example to the Church: Many followed Moses out of Egypt but then reverted to idol worship in the desert, and God destroyed them (1 Cor. 10:6). The parallel with the Corinthian Church is clear—the story shows that people who have begun to follow God can revert to their previous practices with disastrous results. He commends the Church in Thessalonica for having turned away from idols (1 Thess. 1:9), and expresses concern that the Galatian Church will revert to idol worship (Gal. 4:8–11; see also 2 Cor. 6:14–7:1). Similarly, both Peter and John warn their correspondents to stay away from idols (1 Pet. 4:3, 1 John 5:21).

Third, many New Testament writers draw a direct connection between idolatry and immoral behavior. Quite frequently idolatry (as well as fortune-telling and witchcraft, two other non-Christian religious practices) appears in lists of immoral deeds along with sexual perversion, murder, and stealing (see 1 Cor. 5:9–11, 1 Cor. 6:9, 2 Thess. 2:11–12, 1 Peter 4:3, Rev. 9:20–21, Rev. 22:14–15). In several of these citations, idolatry is simply one among a number of sins, but Paul clearly sees idolatry as the source of human sin. He says very briefly in Galatians 5:19 that idolatry (along with other sins) is a manifestation of a fallen human nature. However, his most sophisticated discussion of the topic is found in the first chapter of his Letter to the Romans. Here, idolatry represents a departure from rightly directed worship that results in a turning away from God, which in turn leads to immoral behavior:

> They say they are wise, but they are fools; instead of worshiping the immortal God, they worship images made to look like mortal man or birds or animals or reptiles. And so God has given those people over to do the filthy things their hearts desire, and they do shameful things with each other. (Rom. 1:22–24)

Shortly after this passage, in Romans 1:28–32, Paul repeats that because people abandon God and worship idols, God hands them over to all kinds of immoral acts, which Paul lists in detail.

Putting the New Testament witness together, it appears that the writers, communicating with their congregations, reminded them that they had formerly been idolaters but had given up idolatry when they converted; that idolatry is a repudiation of God that leads to grave moral lapses; and that they should not return to them, not even to

maintain relationships with non-Christian friends and family, for fear
that they will begin its practice once again and be guilty of apostasy.
This brings to the surface a theme that will emerge more clearly later:
The condemnation of other religions is here, as it will be more explicitly later, aimed more at keeping the faithful within the fold than
it is a general examination and rejection of other religions in and of
themselves. The New Testament writers simply want to keep the Gentile converts in their flock from straying back to their former practices by warning them in forceful terms of the dangers of doing so.

There is one last theme to consider, and for that we must return
to the Areopagus. Jews and Christians were not the only voices de-
crying idolatry in the ancient world; some of the more sophisticated
philosophies of the age also expressed extreme skepticism over the
worthiness of traditional gods and goddesses to receive human worship, or indeed over whether they existed at all. We have seen that
Paul seemed familiar with those strains of thought; he quotes a Platonic and a Stoic author in his presentation to the city councilors,
and just before that, the Book of Acts says he debated vigorously with
Epicureans and Stoics (Acts 17:18). In fact, it was through them that
he received an invitation to go to Mars Hill in the first place. What
was Paul to think of people who did not come from a Jewish background and had not converted to Christianity, and yet somehow
seemed to have grasped the wrongness of idol worship?

It seems that his attitude was a bit more ambiguous on this
score, and this ambiguity is a theme that will develop and grow as
we continue to trace Christian attitudes toward other religions. Some
interpreters of his dialogue with the city councilors have taken his
quotation of pagan philosophers as an indication that he was familiar with their thought and perhaps held them in more esteem than
he did the idol worshipers. There is some reason, however, to dis-
pute this interpretation. In the first place, before his conversion experience on the road to Damascus, Paul was a Pharisee, and as we
have seen, the Pharisees advocated a strict separation of the Jewish
community from outsiders; they did not eat with them or interact
with them any more than necessary. In the second place, conclud-

ing on the basis of two brief quotations a familiarity with the whole tradition of pagan philosophy is unwarranted. Given that the Book of Acts tells us that he had been debating with Stoics and Epicureans before his speech at the Areopagus, we might conclude that he merely used brief quotations that he had only just heard in his prior discussions, perhaps from interlocutors who themselves were trying to show him some degree of similarity between his teachings and theirs. Given what he says about the "wisdom of this world" in other places, it is unlikely that he thought much of any religious or philosophical path that was not centered on Jesus Christ.

Though Paul may not have differentiated the philosophical movements of his day from the common practice of idol worship in terms of their value for salvation and proper understanding of God, Christian authors who wrote in the following centuries sometimes did distinguish them, giving the philosophies an esteem that they withheld from the practices of the masses.

The Early Church Fathers

In the centuries following the New Testament period, Christian thinkers and authors sought in more rigorous and organized ways to formulate the content of Christian faith and to come to grips with the multifaceted world of religions around them. They considered questions about Church organization and order, the liturgy, the nature of Jesus as the union of the divine and human, and the nature of the Trinity. Although these writings were mainly for Christian consumption, the early fathers of the Church were also acutely aware that their religion, still a minority within the Roman Empire (albeit a growing one), was controversial and under attack, not just in the form of persecutions mounted by the state, but also on an intellectual level. The skepticism that Paul encountered in the Areopagus continued unabated, and so these writers penned literature aimed at both believers and unbelievers. For the former they composed defenses of the faith that exhorted them to remain within the Church, resisting the pull of other religions. For the latter they wrote apologetic works, works that tried to show the superiority of Christian faith and practice over that of the pagans and mystery cults.

According to the study of the Jesuit scholar and former missionary to India Jacques Dupuis, many of the writers simply continued the pattern already set by Paul: They unconditionally condemned common idolatry and the rituals of other religions of the day, such as Mithraism, Manichaeism, and the mystery cults, while reserving a modicum of respect for pagan philosophy if it led to virtues compatible with Christian values. Most did not go beyond these assertions, but three writers in particular fleshed out their thought with a consideration of what God might actually be doing through the vehicle of pagan philosophy.[6] The authors were Justin Martyr (AD 110–165), Irenaeus of Lyons (c. AD 115–c. 202), and Clement of Alexandria (AD ?–215). These men shared a common intellectual framework for understanding how non-Christian thinkers such as the Stoics, Epicureans, and neo-Platonists stood in relation to God's saving activity. They understood them in light of an emerging theology of history, and they built on the identification of Jesus Christ with the eternal *logos* of God, as found in the first chapter of the Gospel of John. That is to say, they interpreted John 1:1 as meaning that the eternal Word, Jesus Christ, had been active since the world's creation, and fashioned a theological interpretation of human history on that basis. This interpretation enabled them to place pagan philosophy within God's saving activity.

For Justin Martyr, a Gentile Christian who had studied Socrates and Plato prior to his conversion to Christianity, the divine *logos* had been present in human history since the beginning, because it had been implanted in the human heart during creation. God, like a divine farmer, had sown "seeds of the Word" into every person, and if a person were inclined to attend to it, they could indeed see a partial revelation of God's grace by means of it. The fact that these "seeds" come as valid revelations from God explains the congruence of aspects of pagan philosophy with Christian teaching, and the fact that their presence constitutes only a partial revelation from God explains why the philosophers are not in complete agreement with Christianity, nor indeed with one another. In his *Second Apology*, Justin says this:

> It is not, therefore, that the teaching of Plato is alien to that of Christ, but it is not like it in all points, any more than is that of other men, Stoics, poets, or writers. Each of them, indeed, because he saw in part that which derived from the divine Word and was sown by him, was able to speak well; but by contradicting each other on essential points they show that they do not possess the higher learning and the knowledge which is irrefutable.[7]

Justin is not drawing a distinction here between "natural" and "special" revelation, that is, between a revelation that human beings can obtain for themselves apart from God's activity by observing and reflecting on the natural order, and a verbal revelation that comes directly from God to communicate the particular message of Christianity. For him, *any* knowledge and conduct that comported well with the Christian message came from God through Christ (which would make it "special" revelation). The real difference was the degree of clarity or cloudiness in which they beheld God's word at work in themselves.

Irenaeus of Lyons held a similar view; he believed that whatever aspect of God became manifest did so through the Son. Thus, if a pagan philosopher knew something of God by contemplating creation, that knowledge came about through the Son's mediation and revelation and not simply by virtue of the philosopher's own powers of reason. Irenaeus said that the Son did not wait until he had been born through Mary to begin revealing the Father; he has been doing it all through history, as attested by revelations given to so many figures in the Old Testament. Like Justin, Irenaeus brooked no division between natural and special revelation; even natural revelation is not mediated by impersonal reason inferring the Father from observations of nature, but comes by means of the personal Son acting through nature to reveal the Father.

Clement of Alexandria saw the *logos* operating in two ways. As reason, it is accessible to all people, and so all can have some knowledge of God. But as the Word made flesh, it is a personal entity that revealed itself actively over and over again through history without waiting for human reason to apprehend it and reflect on it. This active revelation worked outside the visible Church as well as within it. Anyone who had a philosophical idea of merit had gotten it from the revelation of the *logos*—not just Christians who had true theological or religious views, but all who had any accurate idea about the world at all. Clement also expanded the scope of his thinking beyond the immediate philosophical world of ancient Rome; in his writings he explicitly mentions certain Hindu religious systems as well as Buddhism.

The proposals offered by these three authors thus saw history as an arena within which the Word of God had been actively revealing God to humanity in ways other than simply incarnating as Jesus. However, they left a number of issues in doubt, and modern scholars differ markedly in their handling of these questions. Perhaps the most important question is determining to what extent such true revelation outside the Christian community actually leads to salvation. Were the "good pagans" and Old Testament heroes and heroines actually saved by these partial revelations and "seeds of the Word"? Another question along these lines had to do with the status of the philosophical systems themselves: Were neo-Platonism, Stoicism, Epicureanism, and so on, vehicles for God's salvific activity in and of themselves, or did God somehow make use of them to accomplish a salvation that they themselves were not designed to deliver? A third question concerned history: Now that Christ has come, do the philosophies of the world continue to have any value?

As to the first question, all three seem agreed that the revelations of the *logos*, even though present from the beginning of human history and authentically from God, were still not sufficient for salvation. Salvation still required a full and explicit personal commitment to the gospel of Jesus as the *logos* incarnate. But if that were so, then of what use was such a partial revelation? Clement of Alexandria was most explicit in his answer to this question. The revelations that came to the Jews via the Torah and to the Greeks via philosophy had value as *preparations* for subsequent evangelization:

> Before the advent of the Lord, philosophy was necessary to the
> Greeks for righteousness [....] Philosophy was given to the Greeks
> directly and primarily, until the Lord should call the Greeks.
> For this was a schoolmaster to bring the Hellenic mind, as the
> Law the Hebrews, to Christ.[8]

All three authors further held that if such a Greek or Jew should die
in such an intermediate state of grace, suspended between complete
perdition and definitive salvation, they would have another chance
after death when Christ and the apostles would come to Hades to
preach to them.

As to the second question, it appears that Justin, Irenaeus, and
Clement ascribed no real value to the Greek philosophical systems
as systems. It seems that what they envisioned happening was that
the *logos* already operative in the world and in history was present
in every person's heart, perhaps from birth. A few of the pagans were
willing to be led by the promptings of the *logos*, and thus lifted themselves out of the common lot of the ordinary idolater. However,
without the direct revelation of the Word made flesh before them,
these promptings found expression in other ways, through their conduct and through their thinking. The upshot was that rather than
believing God had somehow created and provided systems called
Aristotelianism or neo-Platonism as means to touch human hearts,
these systems of thought could sometimes become the vehicle for the
logos to find its way into the heart of an individual, or to express the
logos dimly perceived and incompletely believed. In chapter five we
will see that this is an example of an inclusivist theology of the "in spite
of" type. That is to say, God does not save people outside the visible
Church by means of their religions or belief systems, but in spite of
them, and only in a preparatory manner for the time when they will
meet Christ and have a chance to hear and accept the full revelation.

Later thinkers of the early Church sometimes saw the faith of
those who lived before Christ in a more positive light, ascribing to
them full salvation. For instance, Augustine of Hippo (AD 354–430)
stated strongly that all the "just men" who lived before the time of
Christ, beginning with the Old Testament figure of Abel, were in fact

"Christians" in every sense, implying that the revelation they received through the work and word of God in the world was of complete salvific value. In his *Of the City of God*, he stated that all through history there had been two domains, the worldly city and the city of God, and the inhabitants were distinguished by, in the first case, loving themselves to the contempt of God, and in the second, loving God to the contempt of the self. These two cities could not be positively identified with any visible human community, although human groups could serve as signs of one or the other. So, even though in the Old Testament, the Jews were the people of God and thus a sign of the city of God, the scriptures themselves pointed to people who loved and served God outside of the Jewish community. Similarly, outside of the visible Church, the contemporary sign of the city of God, there can be found those who dwell fully in God's city as well.

A third question remains. It is all very well to speak of "seeds of the Word" operating to prepare those who lived before its incarnation in Christ to believe and be saved at the proper time, but now that Christ *has* come, what of those who remain outside the Church? This is a controversial point among modern interpreters of the early Church fathers. For instance, we saw in the previous quotation from Clement of Alexandria's *Stromata* that he believed philosophy had been given to the Greeks "until the Lord should call" them. Some modern interpreters believe that this leaves room for philosophy to continue playing its preparatory role even after the time of Christ. This interpretation depends on a reading of this clause in which the term *the Greeks* refers to individuals who may be "called" at different times even after the Christ event, not to the Greek people or their philosophies as a whole "called" all at once with the coming of Jesus. If this reading is correct, then it may well be that there remain many individuals who have not yet been called—even though Christ has come—and for whom philosophy continues to school their hearts in preparation for their future encounter with the gospel.

To summarize: Although many early Christian authors simply wrote off all of pagan culture as outside of God's grace, a few were willing to see God's hand at work in certain quarters. They took the

Stoic belief in the universal operation of reason (*logos*) and identified it with both the *logos* as God's word in the Old Testament sense and Jesus himself as the incarnate *logos*. They thus envisioned the Word as having been present and active in the creation of the world and throughout human history. The Word spread its "seeds" in human hearts and worked tirelessly through the ages to orient human beings toward God. Some persons outside the visible covenant community, whether they are in the Jewish nation before Christ or the Church after Christ, could perceive and were willing to be led by the promptings of these "seeds" (Justin) or "scintillations" (Clement), and thus discovered true knowledge about God and rectified their conduct. Such beneficial results were not due simply to the pure exercise of human reason, but were to be ascribed to God, the only author of all good things. However, such promptings of the Word, though authentically divine in origin, were still only dim and partial, and did not lead to full salvation; that would have to wait until an encounter with Christ and his gospel, either in the present life or in a postmortem setting. Such a view imputed some genuine validity and value to religious thought and experience outside the Church, but reserved the final act of salvation to explicit acceptance of the gospel of Christ.

Outside the Church, No Salvation

A way of gauging Christian attitudes toward other religions during the early years of the Church is to trace the history of the phrase *extra ecclesiam nulla salus* (outside the Church, no salvation). While the statement is simple and its meaning appears to be quite clear, research by such scholars as Francis Sullivan, J. P. Theisen, and Jacques Dupuis has shown that its import has altered considerably in different phases of history, which has called into question its appropriateness for today.[9]

This axiom, in the precise wording *extra ecclesiam nulla salus*, comes from St. Cyprian, Bishop of Carthage (c. 200–258), in whose writings it appears several times. However, the basic idea it expresses appears in the writings of many Church fathers, such as Ignatius of

Antioch, Origen, and Irenaeus. During this early period, when the Church was small and under persecution, there was great temptation for people to leave it and embrace one of the more acceptable religions of the day (Cyprian himself was beheaded in 258 by order of Emperor Valerian). In addition, this was a period of doctrinal and liturgical consolidation, and the disputes over creed and practice led to many breaks between Christian groups. In short, it was an age during which the Church was faced with the realities of apostasy, heresy, and schism. Writing to these times, these authors used the phrase as a way of warning those who were already Christians not to leave the Church, either by returning to paganism or by joining one of the breakaway groups. It was as if they wanted to say: "Do not go out that door! Outside the Church, there is no salvation."

The fourth century was a turning point in this history. In 325 the emperor Constantine, recognizing that a religion that now embraced 2.5 million believers could not be suppressed by persecution any longer, legalized Christianity. Fifty-five years later, in 380, the emperor Theodosius I made Christianity the official religion of the empire. These developments removed the social and political pressure on Christians to leave the Church, and they greatly facilitated the preaching of the gospel throughout the known world. Under these changed circumstances, the meaning and application of the axiom changed dramatically. No longer a simple hedge to keep believers within the fold, it became a blanket statement that those who were not within the Church could not be saved. Although Justin's teaching about the "seeds of the Word" could still be applied to understand how those who lived before Christ, both Jews and Greeks, might have been touched by God's grace, later Church writers asserted that the coming of Christ invalidated whatever other means of grace God had used in the past. From the Christ-event forward, only explicit faith in Christ would lead to salvation.

This raised two issues that required further elucidation. First, what was the "Church" outside of which no one could be saved? Did it mean the visible human community into which people were baptized, or did it represent a larger reality not entirely co-extensive with or under the control of human institutions? Some of the early Church writers were more charitable on this score than others, and the Church's position became more narrow and rigid as time went on. Augustine of Hippo, as noted before, held that the "Church" consisted of anyone who came to have faith in God, and that it began with the Old Testament figure of Abel. That made the statement "outside the Church, no salvation" utterly self-evident, because the Church was defined as those who were saved. The visible church was a sign of this community of the saved, but was not to be identified completely with it. Thus, Augustine held out some hope for those outside the Church as a human institution, but his followers differed in their reading of the matter. Tiro Prosper of Aquitaine (c. 390– c. 465) held to a kind of universalism, and said that all must eventually be saved because Christ died for everyone. On the other extreme, Fulgentius of Ruspe (468–533), another follower of Augustine, affirmed in strong language that anyone who was not baptized and incorporated into the Catholic Church was condemned to hell.

After the split of the Eastern and Western Churches in 1064, the Western, or Roman, Church's position hardened and narrowed. A letter from Pope Innocent III in 1208 states for the first time that outside the *Roman* Church, there is no salvation. Pope Boniface VIII's bull *Unum Sanctum* (1302) went even further, stating not only that outside the Church, there is no salvation, but that submission to the Roman pontiff is necessary for salvation. This would exclude members of the Eastern Orthodox Churches from God's kingdom. Finally, the Decree for the Copts, adopted by the Council of Florence in 1442 under Pope Eugene IV, specified that heretics and schismatics, as well as Jews and pagans, were not saved because they were outside the Church. This conciliar document quoted Fulgentius of Ruspe almost verbatim, and also declared that no amount of ethical action or sacrifice can aid in the securing of salvation unless one is joined to the Roman Church.

Behind those statements was a developing ecclesiology (the branch of theology that considers the nature and function of the Church) that saw it as absolutely essential to human salvation. A document of the Fourth Lateran Council (1215) directed against the view that the Church is a free assembly of the faithful, asserted that it is the sacrament and mediator of salvation through baptism and the Eucharist, and concluded that thus there is no salvation outside the Church. Those who proposed this axiom in its strictest interpretation often used the ark of Noah as a "type" for the Church, a parallel that prefigured and helped to explain the Church's nature. During the time of Noah, only those in the ark had any chance of survival; those outside the ark were destroyed without exception. In the same way, documents such as Pope Boniface VIII's bull asserted that the Roman Church was the ark, and as such, it alone could convey souls into eternal life. All those outside it were bound to perish in their sins. This meant that there was to be no distinction between the Church as a concrete human institution and the Church as a more abstract community of the saved whose boundaries might not coincide with those of the institution. This is an ecclesiology that Protestantism would explicitly reject, affirming instead that the real Church is that second, more vague and hard-to-delimit group of the saved, and that the Church as a visible, historical human institution was indeed a free association of believers who joined *because* they were saved, not *in order to* be saved. This calls into question the applicability of the strict sense of the axiom within Protestant circles.

The second question raised by the axiom was this: What was the status of those who had not heard the gospel yet, and whose lack of explicit faith in Christ was due to ignorance and not through culpable rejection of him? The answer to this question took two forms. First, as most people understood the situation, such people could not exist. The entire known world, extending northward into Europe, eastward into the Slavic lands, the Middle East, and India, southward into Africa, and westward to Spain, had been evangelized. It was difficult for anyone to imagine a part of the world in which the gospel had not been proclaimed. Thus, the very premise of the question was open to doubt. Second, when a thinker *was* conscious of the existence of unevangelized territory, they invoked the providence and omniscience of God to deny that the ignorance of its inhabitants could be construed as innocent. God had withheld the gospel from their land because God knew that they would only reject it. Thus, there was no such thing as nonculpable ignorance.

Concluding Remarks

This is where things stood in the mid-fifteenth century. We have covered roughly 1,500 years of Christian reflection on religious diversity in a very short space, and so we have necessarily had to omit much detail and draw only the broadest of outlines. However, we do have enough information at hand to make an observation about one significant trend that marks this history. We notice that the very earliest attempts to engage with other religions from a Christian perspective made no broad, general theoretical statements about religious diversity in the abstract. Instead, the earliest writers responded to specific religions and particular problems. What was the status of the pantheon of Greek and Roman religion? How were Christians to relate to the Jews? to other non-Christians? What should Christians do if the meat on their plates had been offered to idols? The reason for the concreteness of those questions is simple: The early Christians lived in a world in which other religions surrounded them and in which they had daily contact with non-Christians, many of whom were friends and family. The problems were real and specific, and required solutions tailored for immediate situations.

As time went on, the need to deal with the presence of living non-Christians diminished. Christianity became the official religion of the Roman Empire by the end of the fourth century, and, as we have seen, later thinkers came to believe, with some justification, that the entire world *had* heard the gospel. The fact that Christians came into less and less daily contact with living, breathing non-Christians had two effects on theological reflection. First, the question of other religions became more abstract; with Judaism largely contained and Islam not yet on the scene, the problems of "the pagans" could be considered without reference to real persons.[10] Second, the Church's position hardened considerably. By the time of the Council of Florence and its Decree on the Copts (1442), one could take a hard line against those who were not Christians because generally this group included no one close at hand, and even if one imagined that there might exist people faraway who had not accepted the gospel, one could at least assume they were not numerous.

As we will see in the next chapter, the discovery of the New World in 1492 suddenly revealed entire continents as yet untouched by the gospel, and developments in European culture such as the Protestant Reformation, the Enlightenment, philosophical Idealism, and Romanticism complicated Christian theology on religious differences.

3

The Age of Exploration and the European Enlightenment

By the time the Council of Florence convened in 1442, all the questions that religious diversity had posed to the Church seemed fairly well settled. The entire known world had heard the gospel, and no one could plead excusable ignorance if they were not part of the Church. The three known groups of non-Christians—Jews, Muslims, and pagans—had had whatever opportunities they needed to convert, and what few unevangelized people anyone could imagine existing could be accounted for by supposing that God foreknew that they would not have received the gospel even if they had heard it.

Fifty years after the Council, however, news broke in on the Church that eroded its certainty about the fate of non-Christians and ushered in a new period of theological ferment: the discovery of the New World in 1492. In addition, new political, intellectual, and cultural developments—the Reformation and the Enlightenment—challenged the very conditions and terms within which theologians framed their questions. Thus, between 1492 and the early years of the twentieth century, these factors called into question all previous theological certainties about other religions. This chapter will explore each of the developments in turn.

The Discovery of the New World

When Christopher Columbus landed in what we now call the Bahamas, on October 12, 1492, he not only discovered a "New World"
in terms of new geographical territory but found an entire previously unknown people as well. In his log entry of October 16, he
wrote of them: "I don't recognize in them any religion, and I believe
that they very promptly would turn Christians, for they are of very
good understanding."[1] The fact that Columbus failed to recognize
anything about their lives that he could call "religion" will take on
significance in the second section of this chapter, but for now we
need to emphasize the importance of his judgment in light of the
European Church's previous assurance that all the world had long
since had access to the gospel of Jesus Christ. With his simple observation that the inhabitants of this New World had no religion,
Columbus, perhaps unwittingly, put an end to that certainty. The
discovery of a never-evangelized people led to the realization that,
for almost 1,500 years after Christ, there had indeed been people
who, through no fault of their own, had never been exposed to the
Good News. That forced missionaries and theologians to raise anew
the questions they thought had been resolved long before: What was
the status of such people? Were they condemned by God for not
being Christians? If so, what kind of God would condemn people
for an ignorance about which they could do nothing? Alternatively,
could God have saved any of them during the time before the arrival
of the missionaries, even though they had never consciously accepted Jesus or joined the Church? If so, what did that mean in terms
of the necessity of personal assent, the sacrament of Baptism, and
incorporation into the Church in the process of salvation?

As we saw in the last chapter, by the time the Council of Florence issued its Decree on the Copts in 1442, the statement "outside
the Church, no salvation" had become a rigorously interpreted
Church dogma. Not only did the Church maintain that no one could
be saved without explicit knowledge of Jesus Christ and formal
membership in the Church, it also insisted that only those in communion with the pope were saved. A kind of "natural" or "general"

revelation might prepare people for acceptance of Christ and his vicar on Earth, but could not substitute for it. But if one was to believe that God is just, and that God's universal will to save all men and women is real, one also had to hold that everyone had had a chance to hear the gospel and make a decision to accept it or reject it. Before 1492 this was a minor qualm, because the known world was considerably smaller than it is now. It could safely be assumed that everyone had indeed heard the Good News, and if missionaries had inadvertently bypassed a handful of tribes here and there, they could still be held responsible by appealing to God's omniscience; if they could have been saved, God would have seen to their evangelization, but if they had as yet received no preaching, it must be because God knew that their hearts were too hard. There simply was nothing to excuse people from personal responsibility for the state of their souls. By maintaining that view, Christians could affirm with certainty both God's justice and universal love in the economy of salvation.

The sheer magnitude of the discovery of the New World shook that conviction to the core. A few scattered tribes being too hard of heart to receive the gospel was one thing; two entire continents, North and South America, populated by millions of people who had not heard of Jesus for 1,500 years was quite another. Surely they could not *all* be unreceptive to Christ? And if they were not, then surely a loving God who willed the salvation of all (see 1 Tim. 2:4) would have made some provision for them, a kind of saving grace that lay outside the normal channels of hearing the word and joining the universal Church. This meant, in short, that outside the Church, perhaps there *was* salvation. But how? Church teaching equally affirmed the necessity of faith in Christ (see Heb. 11:6). The search was on for what Jacques Dupuis has called the "substitutes for the gospel."[2]

Two solutions tried to preserve the necessity of explicit faith for salvation while affirming God's will to save all, but those proposals proved unappealing, and so we can note them briefly and then let them go. The first drew on teachings going back to a difficult statement in 1 Peter 3:18–20 to the effect that Christ went down into Hades to preach to the dead.[3] Based on this, the early Church father

Origen had proposed that Christ's journey to the underworld was an occasion to announce to the heroes of the Old Testament their salvation and elevation to heaven. This provided a seed for the idea that although the inhabitants of the New World had never heard the gospel, they could still be saved by the gift of preaching after death. Natural, or general, revelation might well prepare them for this during their lives, but their postmortem exposure to the gospel would provide the opportunity for express acceptance or rejection of Jesus. This idea fell flat.

The other proposal involved the extension of the idea of limbo to the "just infidels." Limbo had long been seen as a place where infants and small children went who had died before reaching the age when they could make a meaningful decision for Christ and the Church. It was not an unpleasant fate, but it was not full salvation either. Early in the twentieth century, the proposal was made that perhaps the virtuous pagans were the equivalent of small children in conscience, and so also belonged there. This suggestion also failed to gain wide acceptance.

Although the proposition that Christ preaches to the dead proved unsatisfactory, a similar idea held some currency even into the twentieth century. This was the notion that the moment of death itself provides a unique opportunity for choice, and one can, in the last moments of consciousness, decide either for Christ or against him. As the physical processes of life cease, the soul is freed from the constraints of the body and thus is able to attain a level of illumination not possible while biological processes still dominate it. In an adult, this moment will tend to continue the trajectory that the individual established in life, but in children, even infants and the unborn, it will enable a positive choice for salvation, one that is not undermined by the fact that the child has not yet reached the age of reason.[4] Though it seems clear that this line of thinking was intended primarily to deal with the troublesome cases of children who die before attaining the capacity to make a reasoned choice leading to explicit faith in Christ, it also provided some clarity on the fate of any person who died unbaptized, and so could be applied to the case of those who die, even in old age, without ever having heard the gospel.

Another idea that proved successful in facing the new situation came from the writings of St. Thomas Aquinas (1225–74). Although Thomas lived before the Age of Discovery, he, like St. Augustine before him, was willing to consider the possibility that there might be some people alive in his day who had never heard the gospel and yet lived good lives. Because he lived at the time when people generally assumed that the entire world had already been evangelized, he did not think such people were numerous. Nevertheless, he felt that even if only a few such people existed, the theologian must still account for them in terms of God's will to save all people without exception. To that end, he developed his idea of the "baptism of desire." He imagined a scenario in which a person, having come to faith, formed the desire to be baptized, but died before the desire could be fulfilled. Would God condemn such a person simply because the physical act of baptism had not yet taken place? Thomas thought not. He believed that the faith that led to the desire and intention to receive baptism was enough to justify the person in God's sight, and such a person would therefore be saved. This meant that, strictly speaking, actual administration of the sacrament of Baptism was not necessary for salvation, and simply acknowledging this possibility opened a new pathway for thinking about the fate of the inhabitants of the New World.

St. Thomas had more to contribute. He imagined another hypothetical situation in which a person grew up in the wild, beyond all human contact, and thus never heard any preaching. Assuming such a person followed his own natural capacity for reason, and did such good as was in him to do, then God would take note of this fact. This was not to say that such persons would be saved by their own inner light. Thomas asserted instead that God's response would be to send a preacher to that person and make sure he or she received the gospel. If that were true of someone growing up in the wilderness, Thomas thought it must also hold for those who lived "among the barbarians." Putting this case together with that of the person who dies between forming the desire to be baptized and the actual administration of Baptism, Thomas could say that baptism might not be necessary, but some level of explicit faith in Jesus Christ was; the "wild man" still needed a preacher to present him the gospel. Thus, it seems that Thomas's thought goes no further than the prevailing currents of thought prior to 1492: God would know when someone was ready to hear the gospel, and send a preacher; no one's ignorance was innocent.

But for Thomas, there was more than one way to have faith in Christ leading to a desire for baptism. He also thought about a third type of case, in which someone did not know explicitly about Jesus but lived her or his life in conformity with the Christian message. Thomas's cue here was the story of the centurion Cornelius in the Book of Acts, which we examined in the last chapter. He noted that before Peter came to Cornelius, the centurion had lived a life that the scriptures clearly affirm was pleasing to God. Since nothing good in the world can be wholly unconnected with God, such goodness could not have come about independently of God's grace, and so one must assume that God was working in Cornelius's life in some measure. Furthermore, the fact that he readily accepted baptism at Peter's hand after the latter's arrival showed that the "baptism of desire" was already present. From this, Thomas concluded that a kind of *implicit* faith in Christ must have been operative in Cornelius, and while it did not suffice for the fullness of grace that came with acceptance of the gospel and baptism, it was enough for the forgiveness of sins. Thus, both the baptism of desire and the working of God's grace could come about in someone whose faith was entirely implicit, because they had never heard the gospel in such a way as to allow for the arising of explicit faith. Thomas was clear, however, that this was a mere expedient for those as yet unevangelized; after the gospel had been presented to people, such expedients no longer held any validity, and only explicit faith and baptism would do.[5]

As mentioned earlier, Thomas himself never intended his theories of implicit faith and the baptism of desire to be applied too widely; they described exceptional provisions that God deployed only in special cases. The discovery of the New World, however, revealed masses of people untouched by the gospel, and so after 1492, theologians began applying Thomas's theories much more broadly to cover entire nations rather than isolated individuals. Though many continued to hold the views expressed at the Council of Florence that anyone who had never accepted Christ was guilty of infidelity even if they had never received preaching, during the sixteenth and seventeenth centuries, certain theologians began developing the idea of implicit faith as a way of avoiding the conclusion that God had consigned vast numbers of people to perdition for a millennium and a half without any apparent culpability on their part. One hundred and five years after the uncompromising decree of the Council of Florence, the Council of Trent (1547) passed the Decree on Justification, which affirmed Thomas Aquinas's theory of the baptism of desire. In addition, papal bulls issued later in the sixteenth and seventeenth centuries condemned as heretical propositions made by the reactionary movements of Baianism and Jansenism, which claimed that everyone outside the Church is condemned, and that all their works, no matter how apparently virtuous, are sinful.[6]

The Western Church was beginning to back away from its hardline position that only those who were baptized into the Church and recognized the authority of the pope could be saved, and began to consider the possibility of salvation for those outside its boundaries. The sheer size of the New World and the numbers of people in it made it impossible to continue to affirm that God saved only those who had consciously accepted the gospel of Christ and belonged to the Church, and thus stimulated new reflections about the ways in which God's grace reaches people outside the "normal channels." At the same time, however, developments in Europe outside the Church were also changing people's minds not only about God, but about the nature of religion itself, and the events and intellectual currents of the Reformation and the Enlightenment also profoundly affected Christian ideas about religious diversity.

The Period of the Reformation and the Enlightenment (Sixteenth–Nineteenth Centuries)

Increased Visibility of Diversity in the Reformation. Let us pause for a moment to consider what it meant to be "religious" during the

Medieval and Renaissance periods in Europe. Although many aspects of the religious life of the average Christian at that time would certainly be familiar to modern readers, other elements might appear very foreign. Consider the fact, for instance, that God was seen as directly involved in the political structures of nations. The idea of the "divine right of kings" meant that God ratified the head of state, and that to oppose the king was to oppose God. Not only that, but when religion and politics were so interdependent, it was impossible to conceive of a state in which a diversity of religions could coexist; if God is the source of the government's mandate, then any religion that denies God (such as Buddhism), or even has a different picture of God (such as Judaism or Islam), must necessarily be considered politically subversive. Infidelity equals sedition, and no one is likely to "celebrate" diversity. Thus, one can understand why, when confronted by "heresies" such as Albigensianism in Europe, or by existing populations of Jews, society reacted strongly and swiftly to eliminate, expel, or contain them, as we have seen in chapter one. Columbus's voyage in 1492 was financed by Queen Isabella and King Ferdinand as part of the celebration of the *reconquista* that drove the Arab regime out of Spain and restored Christian rule. Not coincidentally, it also marks the beginning of the expulsions and forced conversions of Spanish Jews, with the Spanish Inquisition established to test the sincerity of such conversions.

We must be clear, however, that this did not mean that everyone in Europe from the Middle Ages through the Renaissance was a devout Christian. A popular theory in Western religious sociology that goes by the name *secularization theory* holds that this period was an Age of Faith, and that from the Enlightenment to the present day, society has been slowly losing its faith, or secularizing. Rodney Stark and Roger Finke have shown decisively that skepticism and unbelief were just as rampant in those days as we imagine them to be now. But while Church authorities and the guardians of public morals might have lamented the lack of faith they saw back then among the people, a simple disinclination to religion did not trouble the political waters. The problem with heresies and other religions is that they represented active opposition to the Christian consensus that underlay the political structures, and when new movements gathered followers, they became alternative bases of power that the established authorities found quite threatening. Lackluster faith and skepticism could be tolerated, but active promotion of an alternative religion could not. Stark and Finke believe that our present age is arguably a *more* religious one than the Middle Ages (especially in North America), but it is at the same time much more tolerant of diversity. Here, we are concerned to understand how this inversion (i.e., less religious to more religious while at the same time less tolerant to more tolerant) came about.[7]

The strategy of elimination had worked quite well at maintaining the hegemony of Roman Christianity as long as the Church and the state together had the power and the will to enforce it. The mere fact that alternative visions of Christianity arose in the sixteenth century is not distinctive; such things had appeared all through Christian history, as St. Paul's condemnations of competing Christianities in the New Testament attest. What *was* distinctive is that new forms of Christianity emerged that could not be extinguished, and *this* is what gave rise to the Protestant Reformation, and through it, to a quality and visibility of religious diversity previously unseen. The reasons for this distinctiveness have been well documented. The development of the printing press and movable type made the dissemination of information much faster and easier. (Jacques Barzun has noted that Martin Luther's posting of his famous 95 Theses on the door of All Saint's Church, Wittenburg, Germany, in 1517 was unremarkable; what *was* remarkable was that friends to whom he had sent handwritten copies took them to print shops, and Luther was surprised to find a bundle of neatly printed copies on his doorstep not long after. Through printing, the 95 Theses gained wide circulation quickly.[8]) In addition, the rise of the nation-state gave Protestant reformers places of sanctuary from Church power where their ideas could flourish and be enacted in actual communities of believers. Finally, the ensuing decades of religious wars failed to re-establish religious uniformity. After expending many lives, great effort, and much capital, the religious powers found they lacked the capacity to reinstate even a fiction of a religiously unified Europe. Catholicism and various Protestantisms had no choice but to learn to coexist.

The discovery of the New World played a part in this sphere as well, in that, besides revealing previously unevangelized peoples, it also provided another place of sanctuary. The strategies of elimination, containment, and expulsion described in the first chapter do not depend solely on coercive power for their enforcement. They also require that people not have free choices to opt out of the religious system by relocating, should they desire to do so. Before the discovery of the New World, dissidents had few places to go, and though the new political distribution of nation-states provided some havens for large groups of Protestants, smaller groups such as the Huguenots and Puritans still found it difficult to cast off the pressure imposed by dominant religious groups. However, the new territories of North and South America provided entire continents of land to which such groups could go to establish themselves in their own territories (though we now know better than to believe that those territories were uninhabited at that time). It is commonly noted that those dissident groups were no more tolerant of diversity within their newly established colonies than those they sought to escape, but the vast extent of the land made enforcement of religious (or almost any other kind of) uniformity impractical. If one found life in the Puritan towns of New England intolerable, one had the option of moving farther west and getting away. After the New World opened up avenues of escape, religious groups in both Europe and America had to accept that they could no longer coerce allegiance; they had to convince, or even entice people to stay. This was a step toward the formation of the religious marketplace noted in chapter one.

Increased Visibility of Diversity via Study of Asian Religions. At this point it may seem to the reader that the discovery of the Americas was the sole factor in the opening of new religious vistas, but we must remember that travelers from Europe went eastward to India and China as well as westward to the New World. The colonization of India beginning in the seventeenth century and the trade and mission trips to China and Japan that had been going on since medieval times also did much to stretch the religious horizons of Western Christians. As has been mentioned a few times already, when Western Christendom considered the religious landscape of the known world, non-Christians broke into three main groups: Jews, Muslims, and "pagans" or "idolaters." The first two were the closest at hand and, because they were also monotheistic and closely related to Christianity, not difficult to understand. Jews were the modern heirs of the religion out of which Christianity came, even if most European and American Christians could not understand their failure to convert, since Jesus represented the fulfillment of Judaism in Christian theology. Islam could be considered merely a sort of Christian heresy.

The third category, on the other hand, was rather amorphous, and generally perceived through the lens of the New Testament's condemnation of Greco-Roman idolatry. It was understood as any kind of ritual practice that centered on religious images, and it all had a uniform quality to it, whether it was found in Africa, India, China, or the Americas. The Age of Discovery, however, brought with it increased contact with other civilizations, and as traders and missionaries traveled the globe, lived in other countries, learned their languages, and interacted with local informants and native scholars, they came to a more nuanced understanding of Asian religions, and found that they were far more literate and sophisticated than the simple catch-all term *idolatry* could possibly convey. For instance, Jesuit missionaries in China during the sixteenth and seventeenth centuries learned quickly that Confucianism was a complex literary-philosophical tradition whose literature stretched back to the same time frame as the Babylonian exile, and British colonists in India began learning classical Sanskrit and studying Hindu thought intensively beginning in the eighteenth century. Out of the ranks of foreign travelers, colonial administrators, and missionaries came a new breed of scholar who mediated this new awareness to a European audience that was eager to learn.

The result was a steadily increasing awareness of different religions within the broad range of "idolatry," and, along with this awareness, a growing consciousness of the *alternatives* to the Western monotheistic traditions. As idolatry and paganism broke down into Hinduism, Buddhism, Sikhism, Jainism, Confucianism, Taoism, Shinto, and so on, the educated classes became more and more cognizant of other literary religious traditions with histories as venerable as that of Christianity, and truly different in their outlook. Confucianism in particular caused quite a stir among the European intelligentsia in the eighteenth century. Its nontheistic morality showed to influential thinkers like Voltaire, David Hume, and Gottfried Leibniz that a long-lasting civilization could be founded on a purely humanistic basis, with no reference to the Christian God. It has been argued that the example of Confucianism helped fuel the move toward the removal of religion from the political realm and the founding of the modern secular state.[9]

New Understandings of "Religion." This contributed to a new understanding of "religion" itself. Recall the words of Christopher Columbus when he arrived in the Bahamas in 1492, noting that he found no "religion" among the natives. Can the modern reader believe that this was true, that Columbus indeed found an entire people bereft of anything we might understand to be religion? Or could it be that when he looked for religion in a people, he had in his mind's eye something very different from religion as we might imagine it? We can find some help in resolving this question by looking at the writings of another Spanish explorer of the time named Pedro Cieza de León. In a chronicle of travels along the Andes Mountains, published in 1553, Cieza mentions that the natives he observed had "no religion at all, as we understand it, nor is there any house of worship to be found." Another writer publishing in the same year, Richard Eden, stated that the natives of the Canary Islands went about naked "without shame, religion, or knowledge of God."[10] This makes it rather clear that when Europeans of the sixteenth century looked for "religion," they looked for "knowledge of God" and "houses of worship," in other words, Christian belief and ritual. The identification of "religion" with institutional Christianity becomes clearer when we remember that the word *religious* was a noun at this time applied to those in monastic orders, who had "entered religion."

Increased awareness of religious diversity was to transform the notion of religion and lead to a fundamental reorientation of understanding. To say, in terms familiar to modern readers, that Christianity is one "religion" among other "religions" would have been impossible for Europeans at the time of the Council of Florence; it would have implied that there was a larger category represented by the word *religion* that included Christianity as a member on an equal footing with other members such as Hinduism or Buddhism. In a world in which *religion* meant institutional Christianity, and in which the only other competitors were Judaism, Islam, and idolatry, such an idea could not have even occurred to anyone. But the world changed quite rapidly during the Age of Discovery and the subsequent period of great colonial empires. The religious fragmentation of Europe between Catholicism and a variety of Protestantisms, as well as the growing consciousness of the wide variety of sophisticated and highly articulated religions noted above, made it clear that the world contained a diversity of phenomena that competed directly with Christianity in providing a set of beliefs, morals, and rituals for people. Perhaps all those things were indeed members of a wider class of phenomena that could be called "religion."

An early literary indication of this reconceptualization of religion was the work *Colloquium Heptaplomeres de Rerum Sublimium Arcanis Abditis (Colloquium of the Seven About Secrets of the Sublime)*, by the diplomat Jean Bodin (1530–96). This work, so ahead of its time that it circulated in manuscript only and was not published until 1857, depicted a conversation between a group of Christians (Protestant and Catholic), Muslims, and Jews on their respective religions and ways of life. Bodin, as a soldier and diplomat during a period of religious wars in Europe, had come to realize that a triumph of one religion over all others was not likely, and that such dialogues were the best road to peace. Expectations of triumph had led to a world of chronic religious discord in which "all are refuted by all." Consequently, this book took the unprecedented form of a *dialogue* of many religions rather than a *debate*, and tried to find common truth in all of them, or rather a kind of primordial truth from which all derived, rather than establish a clear winner that would vanquish the others by virtue of its exclusive hold on truth. With this book it began to appear that *religion* indicated a class of equals; the term was no longer reserved for Christianity alone.

Other studies of this sort followed in the seventeenth and eighteenth centuries. The scholar J. Samuel Preus has amply documented how men such as Edward Herbert of Cherbury (1583–1648; another diplomat), the French centenarian Bernard Fontenelle (1657–1757), and the Italian writer Giambattista Vico (d. 1744) all tried in various ways to find the common source and ground for the variety of religions, seeking these by such strategies as looking for the most widely shared beliefs and practices or by discovering the oldest form of religion as a common ancestor of all the rest. As they wrote, the word *religion* came into its own as a broad category within which Christianity was but one (albeit still a privileged) member. This was a far cry from previous writings that had reserved the honorific title *religion* only for Christianity, and failed to see it at all outside of Christendom.

After the work of these writers, however, another development took place. While all the men listed above sought *religious* answers to the question of religious diversity, by the eighteenth century, enough intellectuals in Europe had rejected religion altogether that a strain of nonreligious study of religion became possible. As we saw in the systematic considerations of the first chapter, the encounter of religions does much to weaken the claims of any one religion. When, in Bodin's words, "all are refuted by all," one might adopt the strategy of looking for a larger frame of reference to encompass the "all," as Bodin, Herbert, Fontenelle, and Vico did. But one might also simply decide that all are mistaken, and opt out of the religious enterprise altogether. When that happens, then the question shifts from "What kind of truth do all these religions contain?" to "Why would anybody believe such tommyrot?"

One of the first appearances of this kind of study was David Hume's *The Natural History of Religion*, which appeared in 1757. As the title indicates, Hume was not in the least concerned to find the grain of truth common to the various religions, but simply to trace the development of religion as a human phenomenon in a purely historical manner, giving no pride of place to any religious claims, Christian or otherwise.[11] After Hume, various thinkers such as the French sociologist Émile Durkheim (1858–1917), the Victorian anthropologists James G. Frazer (1854–1941) and Edward B. Tylor (1832–1917), and the Viennese psychiatrist Sigmund Freud (1856–1939), among many others, attempted to account for the appearance and endurance of religion in strictly nonreligious terms. Since our purpose here is to come to a Christian understanding of religious diversity, this branching off of religious studies from theological and religious reflections takes us off our track, and we will not pursue it much further. We will simply observe here that the founding of religious studies in this way helped to further cement the category of religion as something inclusive of many equal alternatives to Christianity.[12]

Science. Another element that helped change the way people thought about religion was the rise of modern science, the conflict that arose between science and religion, and the manner in which religious and philosophical thinkers resolved that conflict. The historian of science Thomas Goldstein traces the rise of Western science to the twelfth century in the cathedral school at Chartres, France, and notes that as soon as it incorporated natural sciences into its curriculum, it entered into conflict with religious authorities. Prior to this time, intellectuals had assigned no importance at all to nature, assuming that whatever happened in the natural world did so because of God's direct intervention, and nothing had any causal power of its own. The main task of the human being was to rise above the natural world of transient things and contemplate the eternal truths of the other world. By simply stating that the natural world merited study in order to find out how events took place, the Chartres teachers were bringing the human gaze down from heaven to Earth, and their more traditionally minded and mystically inclined colleagues wrote vehemently against their efforts and called them before tribunals.[13] This marked the beginning of a new understanding of God's providence in Christendom: whereas before this all events and occurrences in nature were the direct result of God's activity, this new way of looking at nature began to explain the same events as more independent of God, happening as a result of causal patterns or natural laws. The role of religion in understanding the world began to diminish.

Whatever the perceived conflicts between science and religion during the Middle Ages, none of the revolutionaries at Chartres dreamed that the investigation of nature would ever engender a conflict with religious orthodoxy. For them, the study of the natural order simply added to one's admiration of God's creative power and strengthened faith. It is not until the sixteenth and seventeenth centuries that we arrive at the conflicts between scientists and the Church that are more familiar to us: the discovery of moons around Jupiter by Galileo, the observations of Copernicus and Kepler that showed that the sun, and not Earth, was at the center of the known universe, and so on. These created conflicts not by merely shifting focus from the eternal order to the natural, but by putting forward interpretations of observations that contradicted the Bible and Church teaching. If the sun does not move through the sky around a stationary Earth, then how could Joshua have ordered the sun and moon to stand still when battling the Amorites (Josh. 10:12–13)? Other problematic discoveries came later: geological analysis in the eighteenth and nineteenth centuries would make it plain that Earth was far older than the Bible indicated; the discovery of dinosaur fossils would force people to confront the possibility that species could go extinct; Darwin's theory of evolution by natural selection would contradict the notion that in the beginning God created a fixed set of species that never changed; modern cosmologies would show the universe to be far larger and older than the Bible's depiction and that it might have come into being without divine action; and on and on. These discoveries and theories helped establish science as an autonomous, rational pursuit of knowledge that did not necessarily take its cue from the Bible or Church teaching nor did the free rational examination of evidence necessarily lead to conclusions compatible with a

Christian understanding of the world or God's providence.[14]

During the seventeenth, eighteenth, and nineteenth centuries, it became popular to see the world in mechanistic terms; the world as clockwork became a powerful and popular metaphor, for both religious and nonreligious people. For Christians this constituted proof of the existence and providence of God, because a clock implied a clock maker. If the world showed signs of intelligent design in which elements fit together and things seemed to serve a purpose, then there must have been a designer who created all things to fit those purposes. Nevertheless, this represented a highly diminished role for God in the day-to-day operations of the world, as even Christian scientists realized (not always with regret) that a clock, once fashioned and wound, could run on its own without intervention. Robert Boyle, the seventeenth-century scientist who is regarded as the father of modern chemistry, put it thus in 1686: "[I]t much more tends to the illustration of God's wisdom to have so framed things at first that there can seldom or never need be any extraordinary interposition of His power."[15]

The final result of this interaction of science and Christian faith was twofold. First, the place of God in running the world (and thus of religion in understanding it) decreased substantially. Even Christians, when seeing the sun rise or a plant grow, no longer saw the hand of God acting directly to cause those events, as their medieval forebears would have, but the outworking of natural laws producing them automatically. Second, scriptures and teachings that directly contradicted the findings of science were either discarded (the Ptolemaic solar system with Earth at the center) or reinterpreted as myth (the creation story in Genesis). Either way, religion became less and less a factor in understanding the workings of the ordinary world, and, reinterpreted as myth rather than as a straightforward account of "the way things are," much more negotiable and permissive of diversity. If the story of creation in Genesis and the Buddhist view of uncreated world-systems are myths, then they can both stand, something that could not happen if they were both understood to be competing accounts of objective events.

The Rise of Philosophical Idealism. While we are on the subject of reality, let us look at another development in European culture, this time in the sphere of philosophy, a development that decisively changed the climate in which people thought through issues of diversity. Up until the eighteenth century, European philosophy had been concerned with understanding objective reality. To study metaphysics was to seek a proper account of the world as it is. Even the new scientists at Chartres in the twelfth century understood their task in this manner. However, in the eighteenth century, David Hume lobbed a grenade into the discussion that shattered the confidence of the natural philosophers by calling into question the idea of cause and effect, a notion basic to any understanding of things. He asked how we could possibly know that any given effect is produced by a cause. Is it not the case that the terms *cause* and *effect* simply denote regularities that we have perceived in the events of the world? We simply observe over time that event B is generally preceded by event A, and based on experience, we then postulate that A causes B. *Cause* and *effect* then turn out to be mental categories, mere notions, with no provable analog in the real world.

Jacques Barzun has called the work of Hume the "end of empiricism,"[16] meaning the end of simple observation of and reasoning about the objective world as a way to know it directly. Though this development may seem tangential to issues of religious diversity, the manner in which Immanuel Kant (1724–1804) answered Hume's challenge changed the ways people thought at such a fundamental level that it altered thinking about religious diversity as a side effect. Kant's answer to Hume was to agree that cause and effect were mental categories, but to deny that this trivialized their importance. Kant divided the world into two realms: the world in and of itself, and the world as we experience it. In a direct repudiation of all previous metaphysical thinking, Kant asserted that the first realm is forever cut off from us: We cannot ever directly know the world as such. We can, indeed must, know only our experience of it. Our senses pick up raw and far-from-exhaustive information about the world, deliver this data to the mind, and the mind then puts it all together to construct an "image" of the world. For example, our eyes deliver nothing to our minds but raw color and shape, and then our minds put these together and correlate them with past experiences and memories to render the colors and shapes into an image, say, of a tree. We can never know the "tree" as it is in itself; we have *only* our image of it, constructed from sense-data, memories, language, and other mental structures. So he agreed with Hume that cause and effect, and everything else that we can know about the world, is a mental construct based on experiences that interact with certain innate structures of the mind (such as time and space). Such mental constructs are in fact *all* we can ever know.

This inaugurated a philosophical movement called Idealism (because it holds that ideas precede things, rather than things determining ideas), and also represents what historians of ideas call the "turn to the subject." This phrase is intended to emphasize that, rather than trying to discover truths about the empirical world in the way that philosophy and science prior to Hume had done, the new philosophy recognized that our subjective experience of the world is primary and forms the principal subject of inquiry. The effect that this would have on the way people thought about religious diversity is now easy to explain. If, as in the days before Hume, the major preoccupation of philosophy, religion, and science is to discover the truth about the world, then because there is just one world, truth about it must be unified and contain no contradictions; there must be right and wrong, correct and incorrect. Either Earth revolves around the sun or vice versa: These assertions cannot both be true. However, after Kant, with the primary focus not on the objective world but on our *experience* of the world, then divergent views of reality can be better tolerated. After all, two people can have different experiences of the same world, and even if they are couched in flatly contradictory terms, we can understand this as a result of two differing mental construals of the same reality. Diverse views of the world can now be accounted for, and one need not always affirm one view by denying all others.

Pietism and Romanticism. As the Reformation continued

through the seventeenth century, its intellectual focus on doctrines, modes of Church organization and authority, and liturgy brought on a reaction from the masses. People having little patience with or inclination toward the intellectual and weary of the constant bickering over issues they did not understand took hold of the Reformation's new valuation of the individual, but shifted the center of gravity from the individual's head to the heart. This movement came to be known as Pietism, because it declared that the individual's depth of religious feeling was a much better index of the vitality of his or her relationship with God than an ability to distinguish finely shaded theological positions. To use an analogy, it was like saying that what you *know* about your spouse is not as important as how you *feel* about him or her.

Pietism manifested as a variety of popular movements, both in Europe and America. Scholars generally agree that the opening salvo in this movement was the publication in 1675 of Philipp Jakob Spener's *Pia desideria*, which called for an end to intellectual and theological polemics in favor of evangelical preaching, ethical self-reform, and individual Bible study amongst the laity. His message resonated widely throughout Germany and beyond, among people who were tired of the vitriol flowing back and forth between theologians, and who preferred a religious life marked by sincere faith and practical ethics. In the decades that followed, the Moravian Church was established, based on a similar vision of the religious life, and John Wesley was influenced by them after visiting their community in Herrnhut, Germany, in 1738. In the United States, Wesley took his religion, based on the warming of the heart, across the Atlantic, and throughout the eighteenth century, the colonies saw a series of "Great Awakenings," mass religious meetings marked by fervent preaching that engendered highly emotional responses among those who came for revival. This was not a mere anti-intellectual reaction to the doctrinal excesses of the Reformation (who could call Jonathan Edwards anti-intellectual?), but an attempt to bring the heart into the equation alongside the head, to value piety as much as, or more than, theological correctness.

Pietism had side effects within European and American culture beyond the boundaries of Christian revivalism. Some have argued that the set of movements grouped under the rubric "Romanticism" that took root in Europe in the 1780s and lasted for six decades was a secular analog of the Pietist movement. All across Europe and then in America, poets, artists, musicians, and writers began to reject the strictly academic practice of their crafts in favor of something more spontaneous and "from the heart." For example, the formalism of Baroque music gave way to the lyricism of a Berlioz or a Schubert. Individual genius came to the forefront. A new cultural value was placed on the individual and her or his own development and mode of self-expression. (As an example, Jacques Barzun points out that this is the era that saw the rise of the kindergarten, an institution dedicated to the free development of the individual child according to her or his own talents and inclinations as an alternative to the old-style schools whose aim was to deliver a standard "product.") Both Pietism within the Protestant Christian sphere and Romanticism within the world of secular culture brought the individual forward, and in so celebrating individuality made room for a wider tolerance of diversity. People did not have to conform to a standard outward form of the religious life or even hold the exact same beliefs at the intellectual level. As long as a more amorphous quality could be discerned in the individual (be it "piety" or "genius"), these other things did not matter so much.

Both Pietism and Romanticism were also, if not anti-intellectual, at least anti-elitist. Even the intellectuals and leading spokesmen of these movements celebrated the common masses over the cultural elites. In Pietism, a mass revival was valued over the appearance of an influential new book, while in Romanticism, folklore came to the fore as a topic deserving serious study on a par with classical literature. Within Romanticism especially, the drive to master an aristocratic or academic model in art that transcended local cultures and peoples gave way to a focus on the "national character" of local populations as expressed in folk songs and fairy tales. One may, for instance, compare the Baroque music of Bach and Handel with the more fiercely nationalist turn that came later in works such as Bedrich Smetana's cycle "Ma Vlast" ("My Country") and its most beloved movement, his hymn to the Moldau River.

This impulse to celebrate local variations in self-expression rather than a high standard that tried to express the finest in human character as such, also made it easier to look at religious diversity. Rather than try to find "the true religion" that transcended all place and time, people of the late eighteenth and early nineteenth centuries could look more easily at something like Hinduism as an expression of the Indian people alongside German Pietism as an expression of northern European culture.

Friedrich Schleiermacher. We can see the effect of these developments clearly by examining one of the most influential religious books of all time, *On Religion: Speeches to Its Cultured Despisers,* first published by Friedrich Schleiermacher in 1800. Schleiermacher, then a thirty-year-old chaplain and writer who described himself as "a Moravian of a higher order," had been watching the place of religion erode among the cultured elites of Germany for many of the reasons we have already noted: the retreat of Christianity before the new discoveries of science, its tendency to continue proclaiming metaphysical truths in the face of the Kantian "turn to the subject," the weakening of religious claims by the growing diversity of Protestantism and Catholicism within Europe and the accumulation of knowledge about religions of Asia, the confusion of voices within which "all are refuted by all," and so on. As a way of reinvigorating religion and representing it to its "cultured despisers," Schleiermacher did not so much find a new way to present Christian claims to them as completely refashion "religion" itself in a high Pietist form more compatible with science, Romanticism, and Kantian Idealism.

Schleiermacher seized upon the new currents of thought and boldly redefined religion as, above all, a *feeling* rather than a set of beliefs and practices. In the first speech dealing with the nature of religion, he disposed of the idea that religion consists either in a set of beliefs or in a certain morality, because one may observe in the world both beliefs and morals that are *not* religious. For any set of beliefs and practices to be religious as opposed to nonreligious, they need another, more fundamental ingredient, which in various places he refers to as "piety," "religion," or "religiousness." This quality is marked first and foremost by a feeling, an intuition that one is part of something larger, something universal, that pervades the world and holds all things within it. Drawing on the philosophy of Benedict Spinoza (1632–77),[17] he called this the World-Spirit, a divine quality that manifests itself within and through the world. The truly religious person entrusts him- or herself to this World-Spirit, thereby connecting with the whole of creation and all other people. This, rather than creeds, rites, and moralities, is the true essence of religion. Moreover, against the transcendent mysticism of the Middle Ages, Schleiermacher held that such a feeling for God (he used this name interchangeably with "World-Spirit") could only come via a direct engagement with this world and with humanity: "Your feeling is piety, in so far as it expresses [. . .] the being and life common to you and to the All. Your feeling is piety in so far as it is the result of the operation of God in you *by means of the operation of the world upon you.*"[18]

Although many readers may have enountered Schleiermacher's *Speeches* in college and thus be familiar with his famous definition of religion as the "feeling of absolute dependence," they may not be aware that the entire fifth and final speech was devoted to the subject of religious diversity, and that in this speech we see the influence of the new Kantian Idealism clearly. Just as Kant had stated that the world as such could not be apprehended by the mind and human knowledge of the world consisted only of the mind's own constructed image of external reality, so Schleiermacher stated that God, or the World-Spirit, could not be apprehended and worshiped directly. If that were possible, then there could be only one true religion that saw and worshiped this Spirit correctly. Just as in Kantian thought, different minds could construct images of the world that differed from one another, perhaps markedly, and still each be true to the world in its own way, so Schleiermacher believed that the various religions of the world refracted the World-Spirit differently, even to the point of mutual contradiction, but could all still be more or less true, depending on the degree to which true "piety" could be found in them. On examining any given religion, one could discern whether and to what degree it fostered these true feelings of integration into the whole and absolute dependence. To that extent it was a true religion. Some religions did so better than others on balance (Christianity most perfectly; Judaism only in a moribund way), but it did not follow from this that other particular religions had no value; all were vehicles for expressing dependence on the Divine and the unity of all humanity.

Schleiermacher's ideas struck an immediate chord with the European intelligentsia; his book went through two subsequent editions, was widely translated, and has never been out of print. Nor was he alone in recasting religion in a post-Enlightenment, Romanticist mode: In 1802, two years after the publication of the *Speeches*, Vicomte René de Chateaubriand published *The Genius of Christianity* in France. It also appealed to aesthetic sensibilities and the feelings of the individual in promoting a new vision of Christianity. The book was enormously popular, so much so that Chateaubriand had to continually travel around France trying to halt the publication of pirated editions.[19] The Romanticist vision of the noble, cultured (though not necessarily educated) individual, relying on her or his inner intuitions and rational capacities to unfold a particular spiritual path proved a compelling one, whose echoes we can still hear today. Think of *Star Wars*, in which Luke Skywalker, at the crucial moment, puts away his computer-assisted targeting device and follows his teacher's advice to reach out with his feelings. Or think of Rocky Balboa, who, using his own gut instincts, defeats the Russian boxer who was scientifically trained through the use of technology. Both of these represent the triumph of feeling and intuition over a mechanistic rationality, Romanticism over the Enlightenment, the heart over the head. The vision of religion that Schleiermacher brought to new heights of expression and dissemination has proved itself both powerful and durable, and we cannot understand modern attitudes toward religion and religious diversity if we do not attend to it.

Conclusion

We ended chapter two with the Council of Florence, which in 1442 declared that no one could be saved unless they belonged to the Roman Catholic Church and declared their allegiance to the pope. We have ended this chapter in the early years of the nineteenth century with the Romanticist vision of the intuitive individual practicing "religion" (not even necessarily Christianity) to the extent that he or she can feel and respond to a universal World-Spirit. This is a true sea change, and here we must summarize all the components of that change.

The Council of Florence could take a hard line for a number of reasons: (1) The participants could assume that everyone in the world had heard the gospel already, and so had no excuse of ignorance if they did not accept it. (2) Both Christian faith and worldly philosophy explained objective truths about the world, and so could brook no contradictory accounts. (3) Christianity undergirded and legitimized the political structures, so that promoting alternative beliefs was tantamount to sedition. (4) Science and religion mutually supported each other in providing a total view of reality. (5) There were no real alternatives to Catholic Christian belief. Christianity was to have superseded Judaism, and the only other known religion, Islam, was close enough in belief and outlook to seem like nothing more than heresy. Everything else was simply undifferentiated and childish idolatry. Protestantism did not yet exist. (6) Church and state power were closely enough allied that Christianity did not need to tolerate diversity. The strategies of elimination, expulsion, and containment were still feasible.

In this chapter we have seen that each and every one of those conditions and assumptions gave way before new discoveries and cultural currents. Taking them one at a time:

(1) The discovery of the New World revealed a great mass of people that had not heard the gospel from the time of Christ. Their ignorance of Christianity seemed truly not their own fault, and to say that they were all condemned made God seem unduly capricious and cruel. Thus, theologians began proposing "substitutes for the

gospel" that made it possible to believe that people could be saved without even making an explicit conversion to Christianity, much less joining the institutional Church.

(2) The Kantian "turn to the subject" and the dominance of German Idealism meant that philosophy no longer sought to articulate objective truths about the world as such, but attended instead to the construction of mental maps of the world that organized experience and made it intelligible. Because different minds could do this from different subjective viewpoints, it became easier to think that two people or groups could describe the "real world" in very different ways and still be talking about the same reality. This facilitated tolerance for diverse accounts of the world.

(3) The sundering of religious worldview and political legitimation lowered the risk that religious diversity would lead to political unrest and chaos. Once governments began to get their mandates from secular sources such as a plurality of the popular vote or a secular charter or constitution, then individual citizens could believe in different religions without threatening the government. This makes it much easier to tolerate multiple religions within a single polity.

(4) The growth of science, even before the Renaissance, reduced God's direct participation in particular natural processes. As Boyle stated, one could believe in God's *general providence* in creating the world and starting nature in motion, but one no longer needed to believe in a *particular providence* that intervened every time a plant grew or a rock fell. Still later, as science began drawing conclusions that directly conflicted with traditional and scriptural accounts of the world, such accounts were either dropped or relegated to the realm of myth. This aided the acceptance of religious diversity by narrowing the scope of religion in understanding the world. Whereas a denial of Christianity in the Middle Ages entailed denying the very ways that nature worked, by the time of the European Enlightenment, it made no difference: Christian and atheist alike could agree on universal gravitation, the germ theory of disease, the equations that governed optics, and a host of other things without theological considerations ever intruding into the discussion.

(5) The success of the Reformation Churches imposed a new level of religious diversity on Europe and presented people with alternatives to the Roman Catholic Church. At the same time, increasing knowledge of the particulars of Asian religions broke the catch-all category of "idolatry" into many separate and distinct religions: Hinduism, Buddhism, Taoism, Confucianism, and so on. This had two effects. First, it increased the visible range of religious diversity in the world. Second, as the literary and philosophical treasures of Asian religions were translated and made available, it became possible to see a vaster array of human responses to the world than the old categories of "Judaism, Islam, and idolatry" had provided.

(6) The Reformation forever shattered the aspiration for a religiously unified European civilization. The failure of the subsequent religious wars to quell Protestantism and restore Roman Catholic hegemony meant that religious diversity would become a permanent reality. The discovery of the New World also gave a place of sanctuary for smaller religious groups to escape the domination of others and establish themselves in their own territory. However, the very size of the new lands meant that no group could hope to coerce allegiance anymore; dissidents could always move on, as the establishment of Shaker settlements and the westward migration of the Latter-day Saints shows. With more options among which to "shop," the "marketplace of religions" came into being, and religious groups had to sell themselves to a population that could no longer be compelled to belong to any of them.

Besides these particular changes in the circumstances of Christianity in Europe and America, new, more diffuse cultural movements also altered the very terms in which religion was conceived. The Enlightenment of the seventeenth and eighteenth centuries introduced a new role for reason, and declared its independence from tradition and authority. Science (both natural and social) could now proceed on its own way and follow its observations and theories without worrying that the results might contradict religious teachings and scriptures. If by reasoning, geologists found that Earth was billions, and not thousands, of years old, so be it. This rationalism threatened to consign religion to irrelevance, but the Pietist and Romanticist movements of the sixteenth through early nineteenth centuries, by wedding rationality to feeling and intuition, gave men like Schleiermacher and Chateaubriand the opportunity to reintroduce religion as a matter of individual intuition rather than institutional membership, correct worldview, and ritual practice. This new way of looking at religion made it more of a personal preference than a social cement, and, as Jonathan Z. Smith recounts, by the mid-1700s made the words *faith* and *religion* interchangeable for the first time in history.[20] And since individuals (and even nations) could follow their own distinctive paths and still be true to the World-Spirit, diversity was made more tolerable.

Let us make one last observation before bringing this chapter to a close. Although the movements we have been tracing were pervasive, civilizations never march in lockstep, and there will always be the traditionalists and dissenters who refuse to go along. For instance, while German Idealism dominated philosophical discussion until the end of the nineteenth century, it did not drive all competitors from the field. Another movement, Positivism, maintained the view that one could indeed make valid observations and draw conclusions about the external world, and in fact natural scientists went right on doing so despite the philosophers. This movement, while smaller than Idealism, was far from insignificant. Again, although Schleiermacher may have been the father of Protestant liberal theology, he was not the only theologian working, and Roman Catholicism was largely untouched by his ebullient paeans to the World-Spirit that he claimed animated the noblest aspects of all the world's religions. The fact that these developments were not universally appreciated helps us to understand the conflicts over religious diversity in the twentieth century that form the subject of the next chapter, and the variety of theological responses that we will examine in chapter five.

4

New Developments in the Modern Period

The last chapter looked at a few new experiments in theology in isolated places, and saw that within the Roman Catholic Church, the Council of Trent in the mid-sixteenth century finally repudiated the hard interpretation of the dictum "Outside the Church, no salvation." After that we focused mostly on the historical and cultural trends that would set the stage for the emergence of a new liberal Protestant theology as articulated most potently by Friedrich Schleiermacher. This chapter will continue exploring the interconnection between theology and the historical and cultural world within which it took shape. We will begin by looking at the growth of mission work among the Churches during the nineteenth and twentieth centuries, and then turn our attention to other historical, social, and cultural developments. We will bring this historical survey to a close by examining the new theologies that came forward to help Christians understand and account for the variety of religions that continued to confront them.

Missions in the Nineteenth and Twentieth Centuries

Christianity has been a missionary religion from its very inception.[1] In the Gospel of Luke, Jesus sent out the seventy missionaries to preach to the towns of Israel (Luke 10:1–20), and at the end of Matthew, he gives the Great Commission (Matt. 28:18–20), commanding his disciples to take his message into the entire world. The New Testament records that upon the descent of the Holy Spirit on the day of Pentecost, Peter provided the first human response to the event when he stood up and addressed the crowd of onlookers, testifying to God's intention to save all people (Acts 2:14–42). The remainder of the Book of Acts recounts missionary journeys undertaken by various apostles: Philip, Peter, and Paul among them. Throughout the first millennium, Christians went on missions among the "barbarians" of Europe and the Middle East, but efforts flagged from AD 1000–1500. As noted in earlier chapters, by this time European Christendom assumed that the entire world had already heard the gospel, so efforts focused on converting Jews and inspiring lukewarm Christians within the known world.

Columbus's landing in the New World in 1492 revealed new mission fields, as we have seen, and many Spanish missionaries accompanied the explorers as they continued traveling in the newly discovered lands. The subsequent Age of Discovery revealed just how big the world really was, and as greater areas of the world were mapped, Christendom became more acutely aware of how little of it had been evangelized and how many people there were who did not know the gospel. The Catholic Church responded with a wave of missions: Augustinians went into Latin America, Asia, Africa, and the Persian Gulf region by 1625; Dominicans worked among native Americans; Jesuits went into Japan and China throughout the sixteenth and seventeenth centuries, and enjoyed much success, although both of these countries subsequently expelled the missionaries and closed their borders. Protestant Christianity was not active in the mission field at this time; it was still undergoing its own growing pains as new denominations came into being and fought lengthy wars with Catholics and with one another.

Even though Catholic Christians showed real dedication to missions, the limited means of transportation and communication available at the time prevented them from going in great numbers, and by the eighteenth century, missionary activity went into a period of stagnation. The Jesuits fell into controversy and were temporarily disbanded by the Vatican, European Protestantism was still caught in conflicts and paid more attention to urban problems at home rather than mission fields abroad, and American Christianity was still establishing itself on the frontier. Only a few Catholic orders remained active in the field, and the Moravian Church put forward a herculean effort in this period, placing 2,000 people into global missions.

The early nineteenth century saw a tremendous upswing in missionary zeal and activity. The Churches in North America became more settled and began looking outward, the religious conflicts in Europe abated, and advances in technology made possible missionary efforts on an unprecedented scale. The Industrial Revolution that caused massive urban blight and human misery also produced new technologies of communication and transportation, which opened up possibilities for global travel to a much greater number of people than ever before. The entire world had been well mapped by this time, so that few missionaries needed to worry about going into *terra incognita*. American and European naval power forced the reopening of Chinese and Japanese ports to foreign ships and visitors, and a series of agreements drafted under the shadow of Western warships (remembered bitterly by Chinese historians as the "unequal treaties") gave Westerners broad authority to travel and preach throughout these lands. The establishment of colonial power in India, Africa, and the Middle East likewise provided wide access to these lands, and missionaries journeyed without fear into these territories. By mid-century American and European Christianity had a well-heeled middle class that had much cash to give in support of missions.

These new capabilities gave rise to widespread optimism within Western Christendom. The world was wide open, and Christians had the will and the means to penetrate into all corners of it. Missionary societies sprang up in rapid succession: the Church Missionary Society, the American Board in Fujian province in China, the China Inland Mission, the Society for the Propagation of the Gospel, the London Missionary Society, and others all raised funds and sent hundreds of men and women into Africa, Asia, South America, and the Pacific Islands. The sense of *kairos*, that the time was right, was so strong that when the Student Volunteer Movement for Foreign Missions was founded in 1888, it adopted as its motto "the evangelization of the world in this generation." God willing, anything seemed possible. After about a century, the high point of this new wave of primarily Protestant missions came with the convening of the World Missionary Conference in Edinburgh, Scotland, June 14–23, 1910. Several missionary conferences had already come and gone, but those were generally in-house meetings of individual societies or denominational mission boards. The Edinburgh Conference drew 1,200 participants from all over the world and from nearly all branches of Christianity (excepting Roman Catholics and Eastern Orthodox Christians). The atmosphere was exuberant, and the sense of common purpose felt by all attendees made this meeting the first significant ecumenical event in Church history; the connections forged there led directly to the founding of the World Council of Churches in 1948. The zeal and resolve that all displayed, as well as the knowledge that technology and global politics had opened up the world for missions, led the participants to predict that the Great Commission (Matt. 28:18–20) would soon be fulfilled. Some even believed that their efforts would bring about Christ's Second Coming. Trusting in the indisputable superiority of Christianity over all other religions, they fully expected that the religions of the world would fall away and crumble before the missionaries' advance. Charles Clayton Morrison, the editor of the *Christian Century*, attended the conference and reported on a session regarding "The Missionary Message in Relation to Non-Christian Religions" in the July 7, 1910, issue. He noted that the last speaker, Dr. Robert E. Speer, urged participants to pursue comparisons between Christianity and other religions vigorously and fearlessly. This could be done, Morrison reported, because "such a comparison can result only in the enhancement of the glory of our holy faith."

But in the decades following the conference, it became apparent that the religions of the world were *not* falling like dominoes before the Christian juggernaut. Missionaries had their best results when working among tribal societies; among literate religions of long standing, conversion rates were much more limited.[2] The religions of the world proved much more resilient and active than the missionaries expected. Two examples will suffice to illustrate this. British missionaries brought the gospel to Sri Lanka (an island nation off the southeastern coast of India, formerly known as Ceylon) shortly after the British took the island from the Dutch in 1796. Between that time and 1860, many Anglicans, Wesleyans, Baptists, and others came to the island under colonial auspices and worked among its people. In their estimation, the Buddhism practiced by local monks and laypeople was moribund and bound to give way before a vigorous and zealous Christianity. What they did *not* expect was the emergence of what scholars have come to call "Protestant Buddhism."

This term refers to a movement that grew within Buddhism throughout the nineteenth century as a reaction to Christian incursions. Christian missions shook local Buddhist leaders out of their complacency and spurred them to reinvigorate their own tradition. In addition, the Buddhist leaders adopted the strategy of looking at the more successful aspects of Christian life, education, and practice, and they began incorporating those features into their own structures. Thus were born in Sri Lanka, Buddhist social-welfare agencies, printing presses putting out popular works for lay education, and even Sunday schools. Far from being overwhelmed by the missionaries, the Buddhists found within themselves the resources to adapt and resist.[3]

Somewhat later, in another island nation, a similar act of resistance took place. The Ven. Zhengyan was a young, recently ordained Buddhist nun living in the town of Hualien, on the east coast of Taiwan. In 1966 she was in the waiting room of a local clinic when she saw some blood on the floor. When she asked about it, she was told that a young aboriginal woman had been brought in earlier with severe bleeding. When the clinic staff determined that the kinsmen who brought her had no means of paying a deposit for her treatment, the doctors refused to see her, and she died in that place, leaving Zhengyan to contemplate the pool of blood left on the floor after the woman's corpse had been carried out. Within a week three Roman Catholic nuns came to visit her, and began urging her to become a

Christian. Their religion, they said, was superior in charitable work. Christians had established hospitals, free clinics, and orphanages all over the island; what had Buddhism to show that could compare? However, Zhengyan's response to this challenge was not to convert to Christianity. With the image of the dead aboriginal woman in her mind, she set about organizing the Buddhist Compassion Relief Tzu Chi Association, an organization that is now one of the largest and most well-endowed philanthropic corporations in existence. It has a free hospital, a bone marrow bank, clinics, and other enterprises, and it raises billions of dollars annually for global disaster-relief work.[4] As with the rise of Protestant Buddhism in Sri Lanka, the response to the Christian missionary challenge was to take stock of Christianity's strengths and incorporate them into Buddhist practice.

Events thus failed to support the buoyant optimism of the 1910 Edinburgh Conference, and missionaries and theologians retrenched and rethought. Even John R. Mott, the chairman of the conference, reflecting back on the mandate to "evangelize the world in this generation," in 1944 reinterpreted the slogan, stressing that it meant only to bring the word to all parts of the world; whether the word takes root and flourishes in conversions is up to God and the individual conscience.[5] More important, missionaries themselves began thinking about the apparent permanence of religious diversity. As mentioned above, the 1910 conference had devoted a day to discussing the status of other religions, and modern readers might be surprised at the openness of delegates to finding truth reflected in non-Christian religions. Although they denied that any religion other than Christianity can save souls, they did call for careful attention to the teachings and practices of other religions in order to help fashion a truly indigenized Christianity that would not be (in Morrison's words) an "accidental importation."[6]

However, subsequent missionary conferences began questioning the presumed uniqueness and exclusivity of Christianity's claim to be the sole mediator of salvation. The next conference, held in Jerusalem in 1928, attempted to balance two opposing agendas. First, participants were much more aware of the open attitude that liberal

Protestant theology after Schleiermacher had taken toward other religions, and, as people dedicated to spreading the Christian message,
they wanted to oppose this "syncretistic" tendency.[7] On the other
hand, the missionaries themselves were bringing home more and
more detailed information about non-Christian religions, and it was
becoming apparent that they often contained lofty literature, profound philosophies, and admirable ethical standards. In a world that
the participants perceived as increasingly secular, some thought that
Christianity ought to join forces with that which represented the best
of other religions in order to face the challenges of the age. Partisans
of these two positions argued their points of view vigorously, and in
the end drafted and passed a compromise resolution. The controversy continued after the conference, however, and in this way increasing knowledge of the details of other religions as well as their
evident failure to give way to Christianity began to erode missionary confidence that the world could be successfully Christianized.

The continuing controversy contributed to the rise of a theological reaction against Schleiermachian liberalism in the writings
of Karl Barth and Hendrik Kraemer, as we shall see when we consider developments in Protestant theology later in this chapter. Here,
suffice it to say that by the time the next international conference
convened in Tambaram, India, in 1938, the missionary community
itself was divided into those who continued to argue for the unique
saving power of Christianity and the need to preach the message to
all the world, and those who took a more open attitude to the world's
religions. For the first, the issue was the salvation of souls, and Christianity, the only religion that recognized God's revelation and God's
plan to save all humanity, was a gift that all people desperately
needed in order to be saved. Leaving major segments of the world's
population to follow their own religions was to consign them to continuing darkness. The other side, argued by Christian theologians
from India with some Western allies, believed that God had in fact
been at work all around the world throughout history. They could
not understand how a loving God would allow whole populations
of people to die in their sins just because Western missionaries had

not yet arrived. They asserted that God had been engaged in a "two-way traffic" with human souls all along.

Shortly after the Tambaram conference, the Second World War broke out, causing a sudden downturn in missionary activity. When the war ended, a new world emerged. Colonial powers that had dominated Africa and India began to pull out, and a new nationalism emerged in those areas. Missionaries could no longer count on the backing of military garrisons from their home countries or the concessions of "unequal treaties" to give them unfettered access to foreign countries. The very Churches that previous generations of missionaries had planted in these places now called for more local autonomy so that they could form a local Christianity that would respond to the historical setting and cultural patterns of their peoples, giving rise to truly indigenized Christian Churches. In places like India and Japan, nation-building in the aftermath of war and colonialism required that local Christians work together with non-Christians in a productive manner, a necessity that lessened the appeal of any hard-line Christian exclusivism.

The ecumenical movement that took shape in the heady atmosphere of the Edinburgh Conference of 1910 now bore fruit in the formation of the World Council of Churches (WCC) in Amsterdam in 1948. However, the history of the intervening thirty-eight years had tempered Christian mission optimism considerably. Though the WCC did have a program unit on evangelism, it also began to think seriously about interreligious dialogue as another means of relating to world religions. During its 1967 general convention in Kandy, Sri Lanka, delegates began calling on the WCC to inaugurate serious, programmatic initiatives for dialogue, and in 1971, the WCC Commission on World Mission and Evangelism was joined by a new Sub-Unit on Dialogue with People of Living Faiths and Ideologies. Although both these program units worked within the overall framework of the WCC, controversy continued (and continues) between those who believe that Christians have a permanent obligation to evangelize people of other religions, and those who, seeing positive value in other faiths, favor the approach of dialogue.

We will examine this ongoing debate in more detail in chapter six. Meanwhile, let us conclude this section with a few summary remarks. Between the early 1800s and the Edinburgh Conference, a model for missions took root within Protestantism, based on a number of historical conditions. Technological advances in transportation, colonial expansion, and militarily enforced "unequal treaties" gave missionaries unprecedented access to foreign nations, and a rising Protestant middle class saw a chance to go forth into "heathen lands" to spread the light of the gospel. Volunteers signed up for missionary service and went abroad, living for years or even decades among the people in their mission field and getting to know them intimately. They succeeded not only in planting Churches, but also in gaining detailed knowledge of local religions and customs, which they then communicated back to audiences at home. This influx of information helped put to rest the habit of lumping them all together into a generalized "idolatry" or "heathenism," and gave us instead the more concrete and specific categories "Buddhism," "Hinduism," "Shinto," and so on. All in all, the time seemed ripe for mission success, and so a great optimism arose, as expressed in the slogan "the evangelization of the world in this generation." By 1910 it seemed that success would follow upon success, and that the world was well on its way to being Christianized.

Events of the late nineteenth and early twentieth centuries tempered this optimism. The religions of the world adapted to the missionary challenge and staged their own revitalization movements. The Churches that the missionaries themselves planted sought more local autonomy and questioned the viability of continuing the model of Western Christendom going forth into foreign mission fields. As colonialism and the unequal treaties gave way before the rise of new nations after World War II, these native Churches had increasingly to learn to live and cooperate with their own, often numerically superior, non-Christian populations to build a common life for all. The year 1910 marked both the high point and the watershed for an older model of mission work that proved increasingly impractical. In this new world, in which (1) religious diversity now appeared permanent

(2) people in Europe and America had more detailed knowledge about specific non-Christian religions, and (3) Christians outside the West needed to learn to coexist with non-Christian neighbors under a common polity, dialogue emerged as an alternative way of relating to non-Christian faiths. Those who continued to give missions and evangelism priority often resented this new approach, seeing in it an abrogation of Christian responsibility, thus setting in motion a controversy between missions and dialogue that continues to this day.

It is not ironic, then, that the Edinburgh Conference, the very event that embodied this great optimism and gave birth to the ecumenical movement as different Christian bodies sought to maximize their effectiveness in missions through cooperation, bore fruit in the World Council of Churches, a body that came to espouse dialogue as a way of living with non-Christian neighbors. There is, however, another aspect of the religious history of the modern world to which we must now turn: the importation of world religions into Western society through translation and dissemination of scriptures, the arrival of missionaries representing non-Christian religions, and immigration.

Other Developments

Though it was undeniably important, missionary thought and activity was not the only historical development during the modern period to influence the way people think about religion. The same global events that gave missionaries unprecedented access to the world also made the West accessible to others, and this increased people's awareness of religious diversity, not only as a theoretical feature of world civilization but also as a part of their own daily lives.

Literary Activity in the West. Missionaries, traders, diplomats, and colonial administrators went out from Western nations into other parts of the world, and in some cases, their initiatives brought the larger world back into the Western nations from whence they came. As we have already seen, missionaries brought their own experiences and observations of other religions back home, but in some cases, they and their nonmissionary countrymen began very early to identify and translate key religious texts. For example, Sir William Jones (1746–94) was already a renowned linguist in England before he accepted a post as judge in the supreme court of judicature at Calcutta in 1783. He promptly undertook the study of Sanskrit, and, in the last eleven years of his life, produced translations of many key Hindu texts, including the Vedas, the most ancient of the Hindu scriptures.[8] James Legge (1815–97) worked as a missionary in China from the 1840s to the 1870s, and produced such a large number of high-quality translations of the Confucian classics that Oxford University created its first chair of Chinese Studies for him in 1876. The translations are so well done that they are still in use today. In 1881 T. W. Rhys Davids (1843–1922), a British civil servant posted to Sri Lanka (then known as Ceylon), and others founded the Pali Text Society (PTS) for the purpose of producing and disseminating translations of the texts of the Theravada Buddhist tradition from Pali into English. The PTS has produced over sixty translations as well as Pali-English dictionaries and many scholarly articles. These three men are hardly isolated examples.

Perhaps the greatest effort at making the texts of other religions available in the West was the inauguration of the *Sacred Books of the East* series by Oxford University Press, under the editorial supervision of F. Max Müller between 1879 and 1910. This series eventually ran to fifty volumes, and included Legge's translations of Confucian literature, Müller's own translations of several Hindu texts, as well as a host of other translations of the Qur'an; ancient Zoroastrian texts from the Persian; Buddhist texts from Chinese, Sanskrit, and Pali (including some done by Rhys Davids); Chinese Taoist classics; and a general index. This series, requiring the commitment of a major academic press and the collaborative efforts of twenty-one translators, constituted a major cultural event in the West, according to W. C. Smith, one of the most influential scholars of religion in the twentieth century.[9] From this point onward, translation and publication activity increased in both quantity and quality throughout the modern period, and continues apace today.

The fact that translations appeared, in and of itself, is not an adequate measure of influence; such things can be done by a small circle of people for purely scholarly or antiquarian interests without having much effect on the wider culture. It is more significant to find people reading them and absorbing their ideas. Thomas Jefferson and Benjamin Franklin both read the translations of Sir William Jones and his associates in India, and perused the articles in journals such as *Asiatick Researches* in order to enhance their understanding of them. In fact, Franklin corresponded frequently with Jones and once wrote a letter of introduction for him to present to Jefferson.[10] In the early and mid-nineteenth century, Ralph Waldo Emerson and Henry David Thoreau avidly read and disseminated Hindu and Buddhist literature; Thoreau read the classic Hindu text, the *Bhagavad-Gita*, sitting by Walden Pond, and both he and Emerson, as editors of the journal the *Dial*, published a series of "ethnical scriptures," short extracts from previous and newly published translations of Asian texts. In 1844 Thoreau himself introduced the English-speaking world to one of the most widely revered scriptures of East Asian Buddhism, the *Lotus Sutra*, personally translating portions of a recent French edition by Eugene Burnouf into English.[11] The *Dial* had over three hundred subscribers around New England. Familiarity with the literary traditions of non-Christian religions was fast becoming part of the learning associated with the cultural elites.

However, these elites were not necessarily interested in learning about other religions for their own sake. Emerson and Thoreau did not become Hindus or Buddhists; they were more interested in finding a common thread running throughout the religions of the world that would connect and unify them, largely in terms of Christian concepts and concerns. A similar tendency was found in the establishment of the Theosophical Society in 1875, under the aegis of Madame Helena P. Blavatsky (1831–1891) and Colonel Henry Steele Olcott (1832–1907), who looked to the literature of Eastern religions to find evidence of an ancient occult teaching. However, while the New Englanders of a generation before knew of other religions only from their books, the Theosophists sought to make contacts with living members of other religions. Madame Blavatsky claimed to have studied with religious practitioners in Tibet. The Theosophical Society formed a temporary alliance with the Arya Samaj, a Hindu reform movement in India, but, significantly, broke with it when it became clear that the group was dedicated solely to Hinduism and was not as eclectic in its tastes as the Theosophists might have liked. Olcott and Blavatsky also journeyed together to Ceylon in 1880 and formally took Buddhist vows, but the "orthodoxy" of their Buddhism is highly questionable. Olcott returned to Ceylon in 1882, and provided aid and counsel to the Buddhist community as they devised their plans to resist the intrusions of Christian missionaries; Olcott contributed directly to the rise of the Protestant Buddhism mentioned earlier.

The growing availability of literature clearly had an effect in opening Western minds to the presence and value of non-Christian religions. The availability of literature inspired many Americans to journey to Asia in search of the religions they were reading about. Henry Adams journeyed to Japan in search of Buddhism, and other prominent Bostonians of the late nineteenth century also went there and resided for long periods, and some, such as the art historian and collector Ernest F. Fenollosa and physician William S. Bigelow, received formal Buddhist initiation in Japan in 1885.[12] But, as the case of the Theosophists shows, books alone do not necessarily generate real understanding; they can just as easily serve other religious agendas or contribute to mere dilettantism. Another trend in Western society began toward the end of the nineteenth century that would greatly enhance Western understanding of other religions, and would also help establish the religious diversity that we now see. Through both the arrival of foreign missionaries and immigration, the living religions of the world made their way to the West.

Mission Work on Western Soil. By the end of the nineteenth century, increased literacy and interest in the religions of Asia brought about an event of enormous significance: the World's Parliament of Religions held in Chicago in 1893. The parliament was part of the World's Columbian Exposition, a fair displaying artistic and technological achievements originally intended to coincide with the four-hundredth anniversary of Columbus's voyage but held a year late due to logistical problems. Although the vast majority of the parliament's attendees were Christians from North America, invitations went out to religious leaders from around the world, and many accepted. Delegates came from Japan, China, India, Thailand (then Siam), and Sri Lanka (then Ceylon), and represented the Buddhist, Hindu, Sikh, Jain, and Zoroastrian communities, among others. Ten thousand letters of invitation went out, and even when the recipients declined to come, they sent back letters and materials expressing a wide variety of attitudes toward the enterprise, running the gamut from condemnation to moral support.

As one of the first conscious efforts on the part of Christians to engage other religions in dialogue, it evoked the controversy between dialogue and missions mentioned previously. The Archbishop of Canterbury refused to attend or endorse the event. He said in his letter of reply that Christianity is the one true religion that all humanity needs in order to be saved. It could not be put in a "parliament" with other religions because to do so implied a parity among them, an implication with which he could not agree. (Interestingly, the archbishop's letter was reproduced in the official memorial volume published by the parliament's organizers themselves.) Two Christian missionaries working in China sent vastly different responses. From his mission post in Hong Kong, Rev. E. J. Eitel, whose *Handbook of Chinese Buddhism* was one of the earliest dictionaries of Chinese Buddhist terms, excoriated the whole enterprise as a denial of Christ's lordship, while in Shanghai, Rev. T. F. Hawks lauded the parliament, saying that the antagonism and misunderstanding that missionaries frequently displayed toward other religions was one of the greatest obstacles to the success of their own missions.[13] It was, therefore, perhaps somewhat ironic that the chair of the parliament, Rev. John Henry Barrows, explicitly claimed that the Parliament's very conception and implementation were the fruit of missionary effort. The scholarly work that missionaries themselves had done (such as Legge's translations and Eitel's dictionary) had contributed to the rise of comparative religion as an academic discipline, and it was this rising interest in other religions that made American intellectuals want to invite leaders from abroad for public and private dialogue. Nevertheless, the parliament produced another effect to which I want to draw attention. After it was all over and the Columbian Exposition had closed its doors, many of the foreign religious leaders stayed on to make preaching and lecture tours in America and sometimes in Europe on their way home. The tremendous interest their presentations had elicited led them to see North America itself as a mission field of great promise. The noted Buddhist reformer Anagarika Dharmapala (1864–1933) attended the parliament, and returned to America many times thereafter, lecturing in several major cities and receiving financial support from many wealthy society ladies. His presence was an indispensable catalyst in the founding of the American branch of his Maha Bodhi Society. He also spent time in London, and attracted much attention there. Another parliamentarian, Soyen Shaku, from the Japanese Zen tradition, remained in America for a time after the parliament, and though he returned to Japan nine months later, he left several of his disciples in California to carry on missionary work: Nyogen Senzaki, Sokatsu Shaku, and Daisetsu Teitaro Suzuki. The latter went to work in Illinois with Paul Carus of the Open Court Publishing Company. Thanks to his fluency in English, D. T. Suzuki (1870–1966) became the leading authority on Zen in the United States, and his friendship was cultivated by many of the leading Western scholars and propagators of Zen, including Alan Watts of the United States and Christmas Humphreys of England. From the time he arrived in San Francisco in 1897 to the time he died at the age of ninety-six, he had not only succeeded in making *Zen* a household word, but he had influenced a whole generation of intellectuals and artists (such as the composer John Cage and the whole Beat movement of the 1950s).

Hindu missionaries also came to the West in the wake of the parliament. Swami Vivekananda (1863–1902), a charismatic young Hindu adept and reformer, proved so popular in the United States that his speech to the parliament was interrupted by applause before he had finished the first sentence. He stayed on and lectured widely across the United States, on both coasts and in major cities throughout the heartland. For intellectuals and cultural leaders who had known of Hinduism only through literature since the early 1800s, his presence created the first opportunity to meet a living Hindu master face to face. He founded the Vedanta Society in various cities beginning with the New York branch in 1894, which is still active today. Meanwhile, on his return trips to India, he founded and ran the Ramakrishna Mission, a Hindu reform movement that, like Protestant Buddhism in Sri Lanka, replicated the Christian efforts at social service and welfare work in order to revive Hinduism in the face of the missionary challenge. His work proceeded despite his early death in 1902, thanks to the stream of capable missionaries that the Ramakrishna Mission continued to dispatch to the United States.[14]

Other Hindu missionaries followed, of whom three were the most notable and successful. First, Paramahansa Yogananda (1893–1952), came to the United States in 1920 for a conference on religious liberalism, and remained to found the Self-Realization Fellowship. A tireless organizer, writer, and teacher, he set up branch temples and created a mail-order yoga course that allowed people too far from his centers to get regular personal instruction to learn and practice his yoga methods. His 1946 *Autobiography of a Yogi* has never been out of print. Another great success story was the Maharishi Mahesh Yogi (1911?–), who became famous in the 1960s as the guru for the Beatles. He taught a technique called Transcendental Meditation, and was so successful in getting hundreds of thousands of college students to pay for his training course, that he eventually was able to establish a university in Iowa and start a political party. Finally, A. C. Bhaktivedanta Prabhupada (1896–1977) came to America in 1965 when he was already sixty-nine years old, preaching the practice of *bhakti*, or intense devotion to the supreme God Vishnu in his human incarnations as Rama and Krishna. The International Society for Krishna Consciousness (ISKCON) that he founded was something of a joke for a time in wider American culture, known for chanting *kirtans* (devotional songs), handing out literature, and asking for donations in airports and on street corners. However, the organization today is very serious, runs free soup kitchens for the homeless, and has a wide range of facilities and activities.

Hindu and Buddhist missionaries continued coming to America and Europe all through the twentieth century and into the present. Many, like those early pioneers, were sincere teachers who saw potential for spreading their message to a following eager to hear it. In such cases, they were just as concerned as Christian missionaries abroad to create an indigenous Western organization, and so they trained American and European converts to take over after their passing, as when the Tibetan Buddhist Chogyam Trungpa named Osel Tendzin (born Thomas Rich) as his successor to head the Vajradhatu organization in 1976,[15] and as when Richard Baker succeeded the Soto Zen teacher Shunryu Suzuki at the San Francisco Zen Center on Suzuki's instructions shortly before the latter's death in 1971.[16] Other Asian teachers, seeing the success of their predecessors, came to the West with shadier motives, and had shorter public careers before scandal or mismanagement of their organizations drove them from the scene. Regardless of the purity or otherwise of the missionaries and teachers, during the 1970s so many college students and young adults were joining these Buddhist, Hindu, and new religious groups that conservative Christian families, alarmed at seeing their own children abandoning the Church for these exotic groups, began hiring "deprogrammers" to take their children out of these strange communities by force and talk them back into Christianity. A great wariness of "cults" took hold within Christian Churches and the culture at large.

Buddhism and Hinduism were the two main religions that sent missionaries into America and Europe specifically to reach out to those in the Caucasian-Christian mainstream after the World's Parliament of Religions. Islam, due to its contentious history with Christianity going back centuries, did not have the same appeal for this audience, and evidently there was no great love lost on the Muslim side, either. Although invitations went out, no foreign Muslim came to speak to the parliament, and the only representative of that faith was a Euro-American man who had converted to Islam while posted in the Philippines. Islam, as well as other religions that we now find in the West, came in primarily through immigration, a topic to which we will turn directly.

First, however, let us note the character of the non-Christian religions that these missionaries to Western culture brought. Because they chose to speak to an audience of affluent, well-educated, Euro-American and European spiritual seekers, people who, by and large, were disdainful of the "superstitious" in religion and looking for alternatives to Christianity and its "myths," these Buddhist and Hindu missionaries tailored their message to maximize its appeal to this particular audience. For the most part, they presented the philosophical side of their traditions and introduced practices that would appeal to what they saw as the pragmatic American spirit. These teachings and practices could all be presented as highly rational and lacking anything mythological or superstitious. The teachings were portrayed as science, and the practices were said to confer demonstrable benefits: lower blood pressure, increased concentration, and peace of mind. Zen Buddhist meditation was taught as a pristine contemplation of reality and a breakthrough into enlightenment. Elements of Japanese Zen practice that its missionaries knew would not appeal to the American spirit, such as rainmaking rituals and the veneration of the mummified remains of past masters, were carefully excised.

Thus, Yogananda presented the "science of yoga." Walpola Rahula's introductory text *What the Buddha Taught* presents an entirely rationalized form of Buddhist teaching bereft of all ritual, myth, and superstition. The halls of the Vedanta Society's branch temples are fairly simple and lack the plethora of colorful gods and goddesses and the offerings of fruit and incense one normally finds in a Hindu temple. Maharishi Mahesh Yogi's Transcendental Meditation sold itself as, among other things, a way to enhance business revenues by increasing employee performance. (It taught that its technique could also lead to results that would be accepted without comment back in India, such as enabling people to levitate, but it kept this aspect of its teaching very quiet and broached it only to select students.) Only ISKCON seemed to break this pattern, its devotional message being so typical of authentic Indian practice that Indian immigrants were drawn to its temples, and its success among Euro-Americans and Europeans surprised many commentators.

Thus, the form that the imported religions assumed for their intended audience made them much less strange to mainstream culture than the "real thing" the Christian missionaries encountered abroad. They did increase Western Christian awareness of religious diversity as a fact of daily life insofar as the white, middle-class converts were likely to know and to engage in dialogue with their social and economic peers on the Christian side. Nevertheless, the greatest factor in making the presence of the world religions felt in the West has been immigration, which brought in a crowd of non-Christians that dwarfed the meager ranks of Western converts, and also confronted Western Christianity with the more authentic, and therefore stranger, forms of their religions. It is to immigration that we now turn.

Immigration. Immigration brings religious diversity to the forefront of Christian consciousness in three ways. First, when the rate of immigrants rises, the non-Christian communities that come with it can reach sufficient numerical strength to begin building visible institutions; Christians notice other religions more when a mosque or a temple or a *gurdwara* appears in their cities and neighborhoods. Second, when an immigrant religious group attains institutional form, it then begins to import or train religious professionals who, sometimes without having meant to, become the spokespeople and "face" of the religion to the mainstream population around them. Such men and women must learn, like the earlier Buddhist and Hindu missionaries, to speak to the dominant culture in terms it can understand, but because they are concerned primarily with representing their own community to the wider culture rather than eliciting conversions, the presentation of their faith is liable to be much less adapted to the spiritual needs of the host culture's disaffected Christians. It thus retains much more of its strangeness. Third, apart from the visibility of buildings and prominent leaders, increased immigration simply raises the likelihood that Christians will encounter non-Christians in their daily lives. They might find that their coworkers, next-door neighbors, fellow PTA members, or others with whom they maintain long-term contact belong to non-Christian religious groups. Furthermore, they may see firsthand a level of commitment and sincerity of practice that makes them aware that these other faiths are not just entries in encyclopedias or quaint features of distant cultures, but substantial and vital parts of the lives of real people.

With the obvious exception of the native American population, the United States has been a land of immigrants from its founding. However, the patterns of immigration have shifted during various periods of its history, with political and economic situations elsewhere in the world sometimes impelling waves of migration from some particular region into the West, and with periods of acceptance and legal openness alternating with periods of rejection and legal restriction on the part of the U.S. government. Because the immigration situation has been so changeable, its effect on Christian perceptions of religious diversity has varied. During the eighteenth and nineteenth centuries, most of those who came into America were European Christians of one sort or another, and while certain periods of influx could upset the balance between groups of Christians, as when large numbers of Irish immigrants in the late nineteenth century altered the composition of American Catholicism, it did not necessarily entail an increased awareness of diversity. Where non-Christian immigrants did arrive during this early stage, the time-tested strategies of containment, expulsion, and elimination could be brought to bear, at least at times when the dominant culture was even aware that other religions were present.

Here are a few examples that will serve to illustrate the idea. The native Americans were not Christians, of course, but once the power of the newly arrived Europeans to dominate them was established, then they could be contained (in reservations), and their religion could be eliminated (through the sometimes coercive efforts of missionaries to convert them, as happened in both the United States and Canada). When the African slave trade began, most slaves came from West Africa, a region that had known Islam for some time. There are records of slaves who arrived on these shores who were literate in Arabic, knew the Qur'an by heart, and maintained their Islamic morals and practice even in slavery.[17] However, their numbers were never great, and their presence in the overall slave population was too diluted for them to form a viable Muslim community. Lacking a community to support their religious identity and practice, some converted to Christianity. Finally, Chinese workers began arriving in California during the Gold Rush of the 1840s, and many more came to work on the railroads. By 1860, with over sixty thousand such workers in the territory, about one in ten Californians was Chinese.[18] They did achieve some religious visibility as Chinese temples went up in the Chinatowns of major cities with incense smoke and images of Buddhist, Taoist, and folk religious deities, but the language barrier and their tendency to settle in self-contained social groups prevented them from having much impact on the English-speaking culture. Christians tended to deride these places of worship as "joss-houses," and they were often vandalized and burned by hostile crowds.

The Chinese were particularly susceptible to the strategy of expulsion as well. There are recorded instances in which entire populations of Chinese workers were loaded onto boxcars and sent away from a city, as happened in Tacoma, Washington in 1884. In 1882 the U.S. Congress passed the Chinese Exclusion Act, the first law ever passed to forbid any single national group from immigrating. A more serious interruption in immigration came on May 26, 1924, with the passage of the Immigration Restriction Act. This act, which kept all Asians out and set strict quotas for immigration from Europe and other parts of the world, virtually dried up the stream of immigrants, and inaugurated a forty-one-year period during which the descendants of previous immigrants assimilated more fully into American culture.[19] Although other religious groups were present in the United States at this time (for instance, Muslims from Syria began arriving in the 1890s and managed to keep their identity and institutions), the vast majority of people in the country were Christians or Jews. Thus, in his landmark 1955 book, the sociologist Will Herberg summed up the religious scene right in its title: *Protestant-Catholic-Jew*.

One of Herberg's major points was that, during the middle third of the twentieth century, these three groups formed the major segments into which American society sorted itself religiously. Not to be identified with one of these groups was to be outside of American culture, whether one belonged to another religion or was a free-thinker with no religious allegiance. I can personally remember that, as a boy growing up in an Air Force family during the 1960s, my own religious formation took place in Air Force base chapels (which could double as the movie theater on Saturday night), and the military provided three kinds of chaplains: Protestant, Catholic, and Jewish. There were no other choices. In this situation, whatever issues of religious diversity needed addressing within the United States arose in this fairly uncomplicated landscape.

According to Diana Eck of the Harvard University Pluralism Project, the landmark event that gave birth to the kaleidoscopic panorama of religion that we see today in the United States was the signing of the Immigration and Naturalization Act on July 4, 1965, which removed all quotas and opened immigration on a first-come, first-served basis. Not only did immigration begin again in earnest, but the mix of nationalities coming into the United States took on a new complexion. According to the National Center for Policy Analysis, in 1890, 90 percent of foreign-born Americans came from Europe; a century later, in 1990, that number had dropped to just 22.9 percent. The largest number of immigrants now comes from Latin America (44.3 percent in 1990) and Asia (26.3 percent).[20] Consequently, according to the Pluralism Project, at whose Web site one may find updated statistics, as of this writing there were between three and four million Buddhists in the United States, with Los Angeles now the most widely diverse Buddhist city in the world; 1.2 million Hindus; as many as six million Muslims, constituting a larger group than the Presbyterian Church U.S.A., and equal to the number of Jews; and smaller numbers of others: 18,000 Zoroastrians, 234,000 Sikhs, between 25,000 and 75,000 Jains, and (though they are hard to count) anywhere from 200,000 to 1,000,000 pagans.[21]

Christianity in Western Europe has also seen an upsurge in

non-Christian populations brought about by immigration, but the dynamics are somewhat different. The European nations do not perceive themselves as nations of immigrants, and so are more liable to view newcomers as interlopers diluting the native population of a given territory. Nevertheless, their own history of colonial expansion from the seventeenth to the twentieth centuries made possible the migration of large numbers of people into the lands of Western Europe. Colonialism, though by nature a means for one nation to dominate others, still creates bonds between the colonists and the colonized. As the English learned in India and the Middle East, and the French in North and West Africa and Vietnam, the colonized learn the languages of their new rulers in many ways: through mission schools, service in the colonial bureaucracy, and study abroad. Colonizing countries frequently open their educational institutions to the more privileged members of their colonized populations (as when M. K. Gandhi went to England to study law). Even after the European powers pulled out of their colonies, the history continued to impel immigration. In one instance, the revolution that forced the French to pull out of Algeria left in its wake a whole host of former native Algerian functionaries and military allies who were in danger of being attacked as collaborators. They went most naturally to France for asylum.

In other ways, the bonds remained and continue to have effects, perhaps one of the most visible being the Commonwealth of Nations, the informal alliance of former British colonies. The Western Commonwealth countries (Canada, England, New Zealand, and Australia) receive the lion's share of immigrants from Asian Commonwealth countries (India, Pakistan, Bangladesh), and so find themselves with the fastest-growing populations of Hindus and Muslims outside of these religions' homelands. The language of the colonizers sometimes remained in use after the colonizing nations left, influencing migration patterns. English and French served as a *lingua franca* enabling many different ethnic and linguistic groups to communicate between themselves in India and West Africa, respectively, and so they remain in widespread use today. This motivates English-speaking Indians and Francophone Africans to travel to the English- and French-speaking nations of the West. Vietnam, another former French colony, has also seen many migrants go to France, among them the prominent Zen monk and author Thich Nhat Hanh. Finally, mere proximity may dictate migration patterns. Many people from Vietnam, Laos, Cambodia, and other Southeast Asian nations have gone to Australia and New Zealand simply because they are relatively nearby. As a result, both countries have rather substantial Vietnamese Buddhist communities.

Although in recent years the countries of Western Europe have been clamping down on immigration, people continue to enter by means of asylum and guest-worker programs, and those already present often have birthrates higher than those of the native Europeans, and so the numbers of non-Christians on the landscape are still rising steadily. The effects are plainly visible, not only in the establishment of structures such as mosques and temples and in the spectacle of festivals, but also in the increased friction that accompanies the rise in numbers and strength. A prominent news story in 2003 and 2004 recounted the French government's attempts to preserve the secular nature of the state by forbidding Muslim girls from wearing their headscarves to school, and anti-immigrant violence, some of it directed against religious institutions, has grown. Still, awareness of religious diversity is increasingly noticed and even celebrated by many Europeans. In a scene reminiscent of the 1893 World's Parliament, the 2000 EXPO held in Hanover, Germany, featured, among all the displays of new technologies, exhibits of religion. The Thai, Nepalese, and Sri Lankan pavilions included Buddhist statues and art, and the Bhutanese government provided for the construction of a complete traditional wooden temple, with a priest performing services once a day and introductions to Buddhism presented every half-hour.[22]

Thus, as we continue our look at developments in Christian theology during this recent period, bear in mind that, to an extent not seen since perhaps the earliest period in the Church's history, theology was done in the presence of other faith communities within the horizons of the theologians' own lives.

The Roman Catholic Church and Religious Diversity in the Twentieth Century

Prior to the twentieth century, as we have seen, the focus of theological reflection on the topic of religious diversity was the status of the non-Christian individual. The individual's actual religious commitment did not really matter; the mere fact that she or he was not Christian was enough of a problem to solve: Did an individual's failure to become Christian and be incorporated into the Church constitute a fatal impediment to salvation? However, in the late nineteenth and early twentieth centuries, a subtle yet decisive shift in focus took place. Certain theologians began to consider the status of the non-Christian religions themselves as either obstacles to or possible vehicles for salvation. Jacques Dupuis, in recounting the evolution of Roman Catholic theology of world religions from 1900 to the convening of the Second Vatican Council in 1962, analyzes two distinct trends. One trend followed what he calls the "fulfillment theory," while the other bears the somewhat cumbersome title of "the mystery of Christ in the religious traditions." The first theory was somewhat conservative; the second, more open.

The fulfillment theory, which Dupuis identifies with such thinkers as Jean Daniélou, Henri de Lubac, and Hans Urs van Balthasar, gave the non-Christian religions much more credit than previous theologians had been willing to grant, but stopped short of attributing to them any real saving power. Whereas earlier writers (and many of their own contemporaries) saw in other faiths nothing more than demonic deceit maliciously deployed to lure people away from salvation, proponents of fulfillment theory regarded them as expressions of a religious instinct built into the human frame. All of creation exhibits the imprints of God's creative activity, and all of it, humanity included, was designed to point to God and to serve God's purposes. Nature displays God's glory, and, as Christian thinkers had taught throughout Christian history, contemplation of nature could lead to a certain level of awareness of God and God's plan of salvation. In a similar fashion, people were made to enjoy fellowship with God, and so if religions appear in human societies, we should not be surprised. Humans by nature want to reach out beyond the mundane world and seek the divine, just as much as a plant by nature seeks sunlight.

The important contention of fulfillment theory, the point from which it gets its name, is that despite the evident goodness of both motivation and expression that one may find in other religions, *they do not and cannot save.* Just as a radio cannot fulfill its function without the presence of a broadcast and without being tuned to receive that broadcast, so human fulfillment cannot come about without the revelation of God being sent and received. Christianity is the only religion in which this revelation has been given, and it alone saves. Thus, while other religions may have some value by, in a sense, turning the radio on and beginning the search for the right frequency, they must ultimately be fulfilled by the Christian revelation.[23]

The other theory, "the mystery of Christ in the religious traditions," went further. As articulated by theologians such as Karl Rahner, Raimon Panikkar, and Hans Küng, this theory granted to the world religions full salvific efficacy. These thinkers, to a greater or lesser extent, saw the possibility for people to be part of the kingdom of heaven even in the absence of an explicit reception and acceptance of Christian teaching. Karl Rahner was rather cautious in his affirmation of this possibility. He agreed with proponents of the fulfillment theory that the need to seek God was built into human nature, and thus other religions arise in the absence of Christianity. However, he knew that many of those expressing this existential impulse through their religions would die without ever having had access to preaching, and he wondered: Would people who honestly sought God be condemned? He concluded that a merciful God would honor the honest quest, and theorized that some people would indeed be saved; he called them "anonymous Christians." However, he maintained that once Christian preaching became available, people did have to make their choice, and those who chose against conversion would not be saved. (We will look more at Rahner's thought in the next chapter.)

Raimon Panikkar took a more radical view, and indeed has

remained to this day one of the most original and provocative thinkers on religious diversity in a Christian framework. In his 1964 book, *The Unknown Christ of Hinduism*, Panikkar argued for the full presence of Christ, not in individual Hindus, but in Hinduism itself. Jesus Christ, in Panikkar's view, was not to be identified solely with the historical person of Jesus of Nazareth; Christ had been present and active in human history, making ready the means of salvation in and through Hinduism itself. The real task of the Christian missionary, he said, was not to bring Christ to a people that had never known him, but to unveil the Christ they had known all along, albeit in a mysterious way. In this way of thinking, a particular non-Christian religion does not constitute an obstacle to salvation that missionaries must overcome. Instead, one may say that Hinduism itself has a part to play in God's plan of salvation, a part God intended for it from the beginning as a merciful provision for people that God knew would not hear the explicit Christian message for a long time after Christ.

While individual theologians were arguing their case for one theory or the other, the Catholic Church itself was on the move. In 1949, a priest in Boston named Leonard Feeney had taught a hard-line doctrine that accorded perfectly with the decree of the Council of Florence: that anyone who was not a Christian and not a member of the Catholic Church could not be saved. But although in 1442 the Church would have said much the same thing, in 1949 the Vatican sent a letter to Feeney's bishop condemning this teaching and putting forward a more lenient approach. As we saw in chapter two, Catholic theologians began to speak of the "baptism of desire" after the discovery of the New World in order to avoid having to see God as condemning millions of people who had, through no fault of their own, never heard of the gospel or the Catholic Church. The Vatican now put this position forward as Church teaching, and affirmed that, although no one could be saved without being related to Christ and his Church in some way, this did not have to mean actual enrollment in official Church registers. There were special means of relating to the Mystical Body of Christ that God could use when justice and mercy demanded it.

This was not an unqualified endorsement of the salvific value of other religions as such, however. At this time, and indeed still today, the Vatican has been concerned about the error called "indifferentism," which may be briefly defined as believing that as long as one is religious, it does not matter *which* religion one accepts; all are of equal value in bringing human beings to their destiny and highest good. Behind the dismissal of Father Feeney's views was an allocution released in 1854 by Pope Pius IX called *Singulari Quadam.* This document, while loosening some of the rigor of the Council of Florence's 1442 condemnation of those outside the Church by allowing for "invincible ignorance,"[24] still affirmed that the Church was necessary, even for whatever salvation might be had by people who did not belong to it in any obvious way. If they were, say, Hindu, then one could not say that their *Hinduism* had saved them (as Panikkar might put it), but that somehow the Church, as the Mystical Body of Christ on Earth, had done something for them in spite of their professed Hinduism. Choice of religion was most certainly *not* a matter of "indifference."

It was the Second Vatican Council of 1962–65 that became the real watershed in Catholic thinking. In the course of its deliberations, the Church leaders who met together in council decided to compose a document delineating the Church's relationship to the Jews, but the assembly prevailed upon those drafting the document to include statements about other religions as well. The result was the landmark declaration *Nostra Aetate*, released on October 28, 1965.[25] It begins with a statement that the times have changed, and that the global community is closer than ever, and goes on to describe the great world religions, from those most unlike Christianity to those more closely related, ending with Judaism. It affirms, as did Karl Rahner, that even Hinduism and Buddhism, religions very unlike Roman Christianity, were not demonic diversions from the truth, but sincere expressions of humanity reaching for the truth it was created to seek and find. It expresses appreciation for the depth of devotion and philosophical rigor to be found in these religions, and declares:

The Catholic Church rejects nothing that is true and holy in these religions. She regards with sincere reverence those ways of conduct and of life, those precepts and teachings which, though differing in many aspects from the ones she holds and sets forth, nonetheless often reflect a ray of that Truth which enlightens all men.[26]

Turning to Islam, the declaration affirms that even though Muslims do not accept the divinity of Jesus, they still share many things with Christians: a dedication to proclaiming the unity of God; a call for people to submit to God's revealed instructions with an attitude of great moral seriousness; devotion to Mary, the virgin mother of Jesus;[27] and practices of spiritual and ethical discipline. Judaism, the religion that was originally to be the sole topic of the declaration, receives the most extensive treatment. Here, the synod condemned past discrimination and persecutions directed against Jews, saying that God had never abrogated the covenant that God had made with them, that Jesus in fact came to reconcile Jews and Gentiles, that Jews and Christians share a common revelation and covenant, and that Jews today continue to have a special place in God's plan. Furthermore, the text puts to rest any claim that the Jews as a people killed Christ, and lays the blame for that only on those Jews who actively pressed for Jesus' execution at the time of his crucifixion. Other Jews of the time, and all Jews of subsequent generations, remain free of blame in this.[28] In conclusion, the council called not only for evangelization and proclamation, but also for dialogue as a valid way of relating to those of other faiths.

After the council, both official Vatican teachings regarding other religions and the conclusions of individual theologians have tried to maintain a balance between *Nostra Aetate*'s acknowledgment of God's activity witnessed in the teachings and practices of other religions on the one hand, and a steady proclamation of the uniqueness of the Christian revelation and its critical relevance for all humanity on the other. Pope John Paul II, whose long reign has had the greatest influence on the development of post–Vatican II teachings, has been active both in word and deed in promoting good relationships between Roman Catholicism and other religions. In Rome and in his travels abroad, he has met with leaders of other religions, and was the first pope ever to visit the synagogue of Rome. He initiated and participated in the World Day of Prayer for Peace held in Assisi, Italy, on October 27, 1986, and in various official documents, quotes frequently John 3:8, which declares that the Holy Spirit "blows where he wills." The apostolic constitution *Ex Corde Ecclesiae*, containing norms for Catholic universities, states that the study of other religions and the pursuit of dialogue and understanding are to be an integral part of Catholic higher education.[29]

This increased openness has not meant that the Catholic Church has dropped its guard against indifferentism, however; in other documents it maintains both the unique truth of the Christian revelation above all others and the continuing need for proclamation of that truth to all others. In 1991 the Pontifical Council for Interreligious Dialogue and the Congregation for the Evangelization of Peoples issued a joint declaration titled *Dialogue and Proclamation*, of which sections 55–76 made clear the Church's position that the Christian mandate to proclaim salvation in Christ remain in effect. Following the examples of the apostles recorded in the Book of Acts, this document states that Christians have a duty, even while engaging in dialogue with others, to say clearly and unambiguously that only through Jesus Christ and his Church is salvation to be had, and it cautions that "the danger of indifferentism, relativism, or [...] religious syncretism creates obstacles to the proclamation of the Gospel."[30] The document goes on to articulate a relationship between interreligious dialogue and evangelization, which we will examine in chapter six.

An even stronger document appeared in 2000 under the title *Dominus Iesus*, issued by the Congregation of the Doctrine of the Faith. This declaration sounded a caution against any "theology of religious pluralism" that might be used to negate the missionary imperative. It stated strongly that Jesus Christ was unique and that the salvation he offered was universal, affecting all humanity. The declaration created some adverse reactions among dialogue partners that the Catholic Church had been cultivating by its insistence that "if it is true that the followers of other religions can receive divine grace, it is also certain that objectively speaking they are in a gravely deficient situation in comparison with those who, in the Church, have the fullness of the means of salvation."[31] A Jewish delegation called off a scheduled conference in response to the document, and the reports in the secular media bore a tone of alarm.[32]

The storm over *Dominus Iesus* eventually died down, and the Roman Catholic Church has continued trying to walk a fine line between recognizing the operation of the Holy Spirit in other religious traditions while discouraging what it sees as an uncritical relativism that might undermine its own program of evangelization. Although it no longer considers membership in its ranks as a sure sign of individual salvation (or, conversely, that absence from the Church's roster constitutes a sure sign of damnation), it does not concede that it has become unnecessary, or that the salvation of others has nothing to do with its activities or existence. The Church remains, in official pronouncements, the sacrament of salvation, and thus of irreplaceable importance; if those outside the Church enter the kingdom of heaven, such salvation is still mediated, in some mysterious way, through the Church itself. While acknowledging the fundamental necessity of dialogue with other religions, it also stresses the continuing need to proclaim its conviction that God has decisively saved humanity in Christ and through the Church.

Catholicism, having a centralized teaching authority, can speak in a single voice, even if individual theologians and believers mount a loyal dissent to official doctrine. Protestantism, fragmented from the beginning and recognizing no human institution as an infallible mediator of salvation and doctrine, presents a more difficult problem of presentation. In the next section, we will necessarily have to content ourselves with tracing only the broadest of outlines.

112 Social and Historical Elements

Protestant Theology in the Nineteenth and Twentieth Centuries

From its inception in the Reformation, Protestant theology has differed markedly from Catholic theology on the nature of the Church. As we have seen many times so far, one of the most salient questions regarding religious diversity within Catholic thought was the status of those outside the Church. The Catholic Church has always seen itself as a mediator and sacrament of salvation. God had planned from the beginning that it should exist as a gift to humankind, and that part of the way people attained salvation was to join it, to become part of the Mystical Body of which Jesus Christ was the head. Thus, it is understandable that it declared during its first centuries that outside the Church there is no salvation.

This has never been a central concern of Protestant theology of religious diversity, because the Protestant reformers rejected the teaching that the Church itself is a means of salvation. Such an idea amounted to "priestcraft," designed to keep the people dependent on a human institution, and to keep the money flowing in. John Calvin put forward the idea of the "invisible Church," by which he meant the body of people who were truly saved, a body not to be identified completely with the visible Church, which might be full of hypocrites and nonbelievers. For the reformers, salvation was transacted strictly between God and the individual; no human institution stood between them. The Church as a visible human institution was nothing more than a free association of those who came together in response to a salvation that had already been effected by their private acceptance of Jesus. As a consequence, the central question Protestants ask about religious diversity is *not* "What is the status of those outside the Church," but "What is the status of those who have not personally accepted Jesus as their Savior?"

Because the various Protestant denominations lack Catholicism's centralized teaching authority, Protestant answers to this question have varied considerably, but in general they break down into two groups: those who believe that God is free to save whomever God wants, and those who believe that God does *not* save those who make no explicit profession of personal faith. In the last chapter, we saw an early example of the first trend in the liberal theology of Friedrich Schleiermacher, with its conviction that other religions could save provided they put their members into a wholesome relationship with a vague Divine. While Schleiermacher's proposals carried the day in the early nineteenth century, certainly not all Protestants were comfortable with his ebullient optimism.

The Evangelical Reaction. In the late nineteenth and early twentieth centuries, a group of educated Protestant leaders had become alarmed at a variety of cultural trends that, as a group, were styled "modernism." Chief among these trends were Darwin's new theory of evolution and the application of critical methods to the study of the Bible, but they included the liberal attitude toward other religions as well. As a counterthrust, they began to publish a series of tracts called "The Fundamentals," which provided arguments and exhortations against new modernist thought and called for a return to Christian fundamentals. (As an aside, the authors of these tracts became known as "Fundamentalists," and the name endured long after the tracts were forgotten to refer to a much more hard-line religious stance than the tracts themselves displayed.) These tracts were financed by a California millionaire and distributed free of charge to hundreds of thousands of clergymen and religious leaders.[33] Though they give more attention to Darwinism, the emerging field of biblical criticism, and modern trends in philosophy than to other religions, they are not silent on this latter subject. Here is a brief extract from the tract called "The Knowledge of God," by Rev. David James Burrell of the Marble Collegiate Church, New York City:

> The failure of other religions and philosophies has been grotesquely pathetic. The irony of Elijah on Carmel is merely an echo of the Divine burst of laughter out of heaven in response to those who cry: "Let us break His band asunder and cast away His cords from us!" He that sitteth in the heavens shall laugh; the Lord shall have them in derision. The pantheons crumble and the priests die; one altar remains, to wit, the cross of Calvary. It is the sole altar and supreme argument of the true God.[34]

Other religions are mere idolatry just as much as the religion of the priests of Ba'al, who were killed by God on Mount Carmel after their sacrifice failed while Elijah's sacrifice was accepted. Other tracts in later parts of the series stress the need for evangelization and the raising up of "victorious soul-winners," and it is easy to see here the basis for the enthusiasm and sense of urgency for world evangelization that came to a crest around the same time in the 1910 Edinburgh Missionary Conference.[35]

A more sophisticated response to theological liberalism with regard to other religions came from Karl Barth (1886–1968). In the 1920s, as a pastor in Switzerland, Barth came to the conviction that the liberal Protestantism he had imbibed as a student was not working in the real world. The vagueness and openness of Schleiermacher and his followers had rendered them unable to recognize true evil when they saw it; none of his own professors had had anything critical to say about the horrors of the First World War. In 1922 Barth's commentary on the Letter to the Romans exploded on the scene like a bombshell, calling Christians back to core beliefs, values, and certainties, and ushering in a movement later called "neo-Orthodoxy." The full elaboration of this new theology is contained in Barth's massive *Church Dogmatics*, but we will focus narrowly on how it affected Christian thinking about other religions.

To counter the liberal "celebration" that saw religious diversity as a glorious kaleidoscope of human responses to a loving divinity, Barth put forward two basic propositions, which he founded on scripture. First, *only God can reveal God.* By this he meant that all human striving after God is ultimately futile; we can know God only at the time and in the manner that God chooses to grant such knowledge. Second, *only God can save us.* Human beings have no power to save themselves or to "storm heaven" through their own works, rituals, beliefs, or resources. Because we can do nothing to reach God, salvation depends on God graciously reaching down for us, and anytime we do anything whatsoever in an effort to find God, commend ourselves to God, or save ourselves, we only reveal ourselves to be prideful and disobedient. All the "religions" of the world violated these two principles by teaching people to try to find God through their own effort and to bring about their own salvation through useless works. Ironically, even some forms of "Christianity" fell into these two traps. The only true religion was not even a "religion" in this sense; it was the soul hearing and believing in God's revelation through Jesus, and responding with a trusting reliance on God to save, all the while knowing that it can do nothing at all to contribute to the process. Over and against all "religions" was the figure of the justified sinner. Barth summed up his final verdict on the world's religions in three words: "Religion is unbelief."[36]

This basic stance remains strong to this day, as we shall see when we look at the Lausanne Covenant and other movements in the next chapter. The hallmark of the Fundamentals, Barth, and all conservative and evangelical thought is that it places the greatest weight on evidence from scripture, and requires that human knowledge and experience be submitted to biblical critique for final judgment.[37] Nevertheless, even evangelical thought has not escaped the historical developments of the mid-twentieth century. Barth's theology required no actual knowledge of other religions, and indeed his work displays only a rudimentary familiarity with a few major world religions. However, the failure of missions to convert the world as anticipated, the snowballing of knowledge about other religions in books and culture, and the increased personal contact that many have with followers of other religions have given many evangelicals an experience of the other religions that they previously lacked.

Two evangelical theologians who show the effects of this new knowledge and experience are Gerald McDermott and S. Mark Heim. We will be looking in detail at Heim's thought in the next chapter, and so we will focus briefly on McDermott here. McDermott's book raises his central question in its very title: *Can Evangelicals Learn from World Religions?* Though he maintains the core evangelical positions of the primacy of scripture and the necessity to evangelize the world, he raises the possibility that other religions may in fact contain valid revelations from God from which Christians can learn. He cautions that approaching other religions in such a way will lead to a specifically Christian interpretation of them that their own adherents would consider distorted, but he is willing to propose that a serious study of other systems of doctrine and practice can teach the faithful Christian to see his or her own faith in a new and illuminating light. He concludes that although God does not save through other religions, God does speak through them. In this way McDermott speaks to many evangelical and conservative Christians who, with more information about other religions under their belts, are beginning to look at them in a more nuanced manner.

The Continuation of the Liberal Tradition. Although evangelicals maintain that there is no way in which human beings may be saved except through personal faith in Jesus, a more liberal tradition maintains that a loving God must make provision for the salvation of all people, even those who do not accept it through Jesus Christ by name. Schubert Ogden says that they arrive at this conclusion because they are more willing to put their own observations and experience of non-Christians into the hopper when considering the question. Ogden follows the venerable Protestant teaching that only God can know who is and is not saved, because salvation comes at God's initiative. It is hubris, therefore, to think that any theologian can, on some principle or another, say who belongs in the company of the saved.[38] He further criticizes the restrictive view of salvation found among evangelicals as inappropriate to Jesus Christ. If a large number of human beings has been left in their sins through no fault of their own, that would be an evil. Because all Christians believe that only God sets the terms of salvation, then the condemnation of such people would rest with God. This makes God responsible for an evil that Ogden says is incompatible with our notion that God is wholly good.[39] In his argument Ogden gives voice to the misgivings of many Christians who have wondered about the fate of those who have never encountered the gospel and so cannot be held responsible for the fact that they have never personally accepted Jesus. Ogden thus claims that the position that fits best with Protestant thought is neither a rigid exclusivism nor an indifferent relativism, but simply an acceptance of the possibility that God may, by free grace, save people outside the boundaries by which we try to define who is in and who is out. We need not even be able to identify such people; we need only acknowledge that it is, in principle, possible.[40]

Other theologians have made the surprising move of turning Barth's argument that "religion is unbelief" into a basis for accepting the possibility Ogden lays out. David Lochhead, in his *The Dialogical Imperative*, claims to follow exactly Barth's dictum that any religion that attempts to "storm heaven" by human contrivances cannot be the true religion, and that Christianity is no exception to that principle. However, Lochhead wonders why such a principle may not apply across the board? If the "true religion" is the one in which individuals realize their own helplessness and adopt an attitude of complete trust, and if such a "true religion" cannot be equated with *any* of the entities that we call the "world religions" (including Christianity), then it follows that Barth's "justified sinner" could be found both within and outside the earthly Church, and may well include individuals who have never formally accepted the gospel. Barth's divorce of salvation from religious affiliation thus becomes a vehicle for opening up new ways of seeing people outside one's Christian faith. He points out that Barth himself had provided criteria for authenticating God's activity outside of the Bible and the Church, and recommends that these be applied to see if real grace might be active beyond our usual boundaries.[41]

Many Protestant theologians have weighed in on the topic, seeking in various ways to demonstrate that God saves people in other religions, and theorizing about how Christians might account for this, and how such extramural salvation might be harmonized with the witness of the Bible and the long tradition of Church teaching. It would be tedious to survey all these writings here. Instead, we will end this section by asking whether such liberal theologies have affected the life of institutional Protestant Churches to any great extent. To this, we would have to say the answer is yes, at least among some Protestant denominations. We will take the Anglican Communion as an example.

We will recall that the Anglican Communion started from a very

conservative position; we have already seen that, in 1893, the Archbishop of Canterbury responded to his invitation to attend the
World's Parliament of Religions with a harshly worded refusal, stating that he was bound to reject any forum that made Christianity
just one among other religions. If we look over the resolutions that
have been passed by the Lambeth Conferences over the past century,
we note that this pattern of thought was embraced by the assembled
bishops until about the middle of the twentieth century.

At the time of the first Lambeth Conference, in 1867, the
Church of England was the established Church of a country that had
in its possession a vast colonial empire, and so the main concern of
this and subsequent conferences was with missionary work, the posting of bishops into new mission fields (unabashedly called "heathen
lands" in the resolutions of the 1888 Conference), and the limits
within which the Christian faith might be adapted to local culture.
One may search through the resolutions of all the Lambeth Conferences from 1867 to 1958 without finding any indication that the
bishops felt a need to enter into dialogue with or gather more information about other religions. Resolution 8 of the 1867 Conference
expresses a perfect confidence in the completeness and sufficiency
of the Christian faith, and authorizes only the most minimal adjustments to local conditions:

> That, in order to the binding of the Churches of our colonial
> empire and the missionary Churches beyond them in the clos-
> est union with the Mother-Church, it is necessary that they re-
> ceive and maintain without alteration the standards of faith
> and doctrine as now in use in that Church. That, nevertheless,
> each province should have the right to make such adaptations
> and additions to the services of the Church as its peculiar cir-
> cumstances may require. Provided, that no change or addition
> be made inconsistent with the spirit and principles of the
> Book of Common Prayer, and that all such changes be liable
> to revision by any synod of the Anglican Communion in
> which the said province shall be represented.[42]

Resolution 14 of the 1897 conference runs in a similar vein:

> That while we heartily thank God for the missionary zeal which he has kindled in our Communion, and for the abundant blessing bestowed on such work as has been done, we recommend that prompt and continuous efforts be made to arouse the Church to recognise as a necessary and constant element in the spiritual life of the Body, and of each member of it, the fulfilment of our Lord's great commission to evangelise all nations.

This resolution was followed immediately by Resolution 15, which criticized Christian interest in other religions:

> That the tendency of many English-speaking Christians to entertain an exaggerated opinion of the excellences of Hinduism and Buddhism, and to ignore the fact that Jesus Christ alone has been constituted Saviour and King of mankind, should be vigorously corrected.

This resolution, remember, was passed right after the World's Parliament in 1893, when Anagarika Dharmapala and Swami Vivekananda were traveling extensively throughout Christendom. The next two resolutions, 16 and 17, recommend vigorous evangelization campaigns among Jews and Muslims (here called "Mohammedans").

This is largely where things remained through the first half of the twentieth century. Subsequent Lambeth Conferences called for more missionaries to take to the field, and for the rapid indigenization and independence of newly planted Churches and dioceses. The questions appear to have remained settled for a few decades, as evidenced by the fact that the 1930 and 1948 conferences offered no resolutions on the subject of either missions or relations with other religions at all. The 1958 Lambeth Conference passed several resolutions under the heading of "missionary appeal," but these show a shift from previous resolutions. Though calls for dialogue with other religions are still lacking, the strong call for the Church to send "workers into the field" has become much attenuated, and the resolutions offer mere bland calls for stewardship to support the

Church's missions, for increased efforts in literary translation, and for an abatement of governmental restrictions on missionary activity in overseas fields. By this late date, the age of colonialism had ended, and so the language of caring for "our colonial holdings" is gone. The local diocese has become the primary agent of overseas missions, and the conference calls for the traditional English and American missionary societies to avoid competing with the local bishop in the matter of evangelism.

The 1968 Lambeth Conference departed drastically from all previous conferences in the matter of relations with other religions. During this decade, the same one in which the Second Vatican Council opened the door to positive relations with other faiths, the assembled bishops passed Resolution 11:

> It is the conviction of the Conference that, in their obedience to Christ's mission and command and in their obligation towards the contemporary world, the Christian Churches must endeavour such positive relationship to the different religions of men, and to the doubt and denial of faith, as will (a) set forward the common unity of mankind and a common participation in its present history; (b) encourage Christians to increasing co-operation with men of other faiths in the fields of economic, social, and moral action; (c) call Christians not only to study other faiths in their own seriousness but also to study unbelief in its real quality.

This was followed immediately by Resolution 12, which called for interreligious dialogue:

> The Conference recommends a renewed and vigorous implementation of the task of inter-religious dialogue already set in hand in the study centres organised by the World Council of Churches and other bodies, and urges increased Anglican support both in the seconding of personnel and in the provision of money. It also commends similar assistance for dialogue with Marxists and those who profess no religious faith.

These sentiments were repeated in Resolution 37 of the 1978 conference and in Resolutions 20 and 21 of the 1988 conference. Resolution 20 was particularly interesting because it attempted, in a few brief statements, to define the relationship between dialogue and mission: "Acknowledging that such dialogue, which is not a substitute for evangelism, may be a contribution in helping people of different faiths to make common cause in resolving issues of peacemaking, social justice, and religious liberty, we further commend each province to initiate such dialogue in partnership with other Christian Churches where appropriate."

In response to the call of Resolution 20, the Anglican Communion founded the Network for Inter-Faith Concerns (NIFCON) in 1993, as a way of institutionalizing the practice of interreligious dialogue alongside the agencies more concerned with traditional missionary work. The interrelationship of these two areas continued as a vital question in the 1998 Lambeth Conference, at whose request Bishop Michael Nazir-Ali prepared the study document "Embassy, Hospitality, and Dialogue." This essay sought, in an extended way, to give the history of interreligious encounter from Old Testament times through the modern Church's colonial experience, to lay out a trinitarian theology of dialogue, to define the proper relationship between dialogue and witness, and to set proper limits to Christian interactions with people of other faiths in the modern situation. We will return to these issues in chapter six.

The timing of the change in Anglican attitudes during the 1960s coincides with the liberalization of Catholic thought during the Second Vatican Council, and with the establishment of the dialogue unit within the World Council of Churches. The collapse of the great colonial empires, immigration, academic study and teaching about other religions, and all the other cultural and historical trends we have been tracing, all made a strict exclusivism increasingly difficult to maintain, and the shrinking of the global village made cooperation across national, cultural, and religious lines imperative. The times called forth a more open theology, and made the old missionary triumphalism of the Edinburgh Conference of 1910 more and more untenable. But we are not quite finished yet.

Other Developments

Before concluding this survey, we must note two further trends in Christian thinking about other religions that transcend the Protestant-Catholic division. The first has to do with the *who* of theology, the other with the *what*.

Emergence of Non-Western Theologians. By the middle of the twentieth century, European and American Christians no longer monopolized the writing of theology. As the Lambeth Conference documents show, throughout the century the Churches initially founded by missionaries had become both indigenous and self-governing, with their own educational institutions and agendas. Places like the United Theological College in Bangalore, India, and the Tainan Theological Seminary in Taiwan now employ very few Western faculty, and the work being done in those places caters much more to local needs.

That has sometimes led to a degree of conflict with the mother institutions. Within Roman Catholicism, for example, the Federation of Asian Bishops' Conferences (FABC), an organization of Asian bishops, has had a long-running disagreement with the Vatican over the means and ends of interreligious dialogue. While the Vatican, in documents such as *Dominus Iesus* and *Redemptoris Missio*, has tried to maintain the "objective deficiency" of other religions and the ongoing need for explicit proclamation of Jesus Christ throughout the world, the FABC has been urging more dialogue and cooperation with other faiths. These bishops point out that they generally tend churches in places where Christians are a minority, where many Christians are still recent converts, and where the converts generally have family members in the dominant faiths. In a highly pluralistic culture in which they lack political clout and are sometimes even persecuted, and where memories of Christian colonial occupation are still fresh, overly bold statements about the superiority of the Christian faith are simply ill advised.

More positively, however, these Churches, living side by side with indigenous religious traditions and their long histories of profound thought and lofty mystical experience, are more likely to see the strengths of their neighbors' religions up close, and because they share a common cultural and linguistic background, to have a more finely nuanced appreciation of their heritage and significance than would Western observers. Even in places around Asia where Christians are more accepted and do not feel the need for dialogue as part of a strategy for survival, churchgoers attend to the panoply of faiths of which they form a vital part, and they would seek dialogue and cooperation with their neighbors and family simply because they *are* neighbors and family. Thus, theologians such as M. M. Thomas and Paul Devanandan of India and Seiichi Yagi of Japan have made their own voices heard, presenting Christianity in a different key than their western counterparts. They have also contributed to the other emergent trend, which we will now note briefly.

Emergence of the "Theology of World Religions" and "Comparative Theology." In a sense this entire chapter has been about the emergence of the "theology of world religions." The shift from concern over the status of individual non-Christians to questions over the status of other religions as such has opened a new area of theological inquiry that has gained self-consciousness only within the last couple of decades. Theologians are asking: What do we, as Christians, make of other faiths? Are they deceptions luring people away from the truth? Or is it possible that their existence and perdurance have been part of God's plan from the very beginning? If so, what purpose does God have in mind for them? How do they contribute to the salvation of human beings? We will examine such questions more closely in the next chapter.

Even more recent has been the emergence of "comparative theology," and it is in this area that scholarship in other religions has made a contribution. In the past a theologian such as Karl Barth could propose a theology of world religions without any detailed knowledge of the actual teachings and practices of other faiths, but comparative theology requires a great deal of knowledge about other religions. This new method in theology takes the very core concepts found in other religions and investigates the possibility of their application to Christian questions. For example, the Japanese Protestant theologian Seiichi Yagi has taken a set of very abstract concepts from a particular school of Japanese Zen Buddhism and applied them to the Christian doctrine of the Trinity.[43] The Episcopal priest and theologian John Keenan, drawing on a deep knowledge of two major forms of Mahayana Buddhist philosophy (Madhyamika and Yogacara), has suggested new ways of construing Christian truth and the experience of the self,[44] and has used these concepts as the basis for a commentary on the Gospel of Mark.[45] The Jesuit scholar Francis X. Clooney has made use of Hindu and Buddhist concepts to help shed new light on aspects of Christian metaphysics and devotional practices.[46] Such studies draw on deep and extensive learning about other religions, and make it available as a resource for theological reflection within Christianity, often revealing new and unexpected angles and approaches to traditional theological questions.

Conclusions

To sum up, we see that the currents of modern political and religious history have produced similar shifts in theology in several branches of Christianity. In the middle of the nineteenth century, most Christians in the West hewed to what we today might consider a rather hard line: Christianity was the one true religion, and Christian ecclesial bodies were under the obligation of the Great Commission to proclaim Christ to the world. However, by this time some cracks had appeared in this consensus. Schleiermacher's liberal approach had many followers, and the Catholic Church, hardly a bastion of liberalism at that time, was beginning to soften its blanket condemnation of other faiths. As the first half of the twentieth century passed, the world religions had pushed back against Christian missions, and their own missionaries had begun migrating to the West to make their cases. A sea change took place in the 1960s as the colonial experience of the Western powers, once a source of pride, became more of a problem as the West interacted with its former colonies. In addition, increased mobility and migration put

Christians into much greater daily contact with non-Christians than ever before. Finally, the churches that had taken root as a result of past missionary effort became autonomous and began producing their own theologians who sought to make Christianity work in situations where it was a minority, sometimes a persecuted one, and in which religious diversity might be found even at the level of the family.

Looking Back, Looking Ahead

We have now come to the end of our survey of Christian attitudes toward and relationships with other religions from Bible times to the present, and it is time to take a moment to see what we have gained.

In the introduction I promised the reader that this study would provide "conceptual tools" for their own reflections on religious diversity and their Christian faith. At this point it may appear that historically, Christian scriptures, theologians, and institutions have taken a wide variety of stances toward other religions, from the hard exclusivism of the Council of Florence to the more open attitudes of both the early Church and the late twentieth century, and this may make the lessons of history hard to discern. However, what stands out clearly in this patchwork of attitudes and arguments is the connection between the theology of any given period and the historical and cultural situation in which theology found itself. If the early Church seemed a bit more open to other faiths than it would be in the mid-fifteenth century, we must remember that the Church was a minority group (albeit a rapidly growing one) within the Roman Empire, and consisted largely of new converts. They lived in a situation of great religious diversity, and had close daily contact with people of other faiths who might even have been members of their own families. By 1442 the Western world *was* Christendom, people believed that the entire world had been evangelized, and one might pass an entire lifetime without ever meeting a non-Christian.

The year 1492 marked a watershed, for Columbus's discovery of the New World shattered the confidence that the world had long since been evangelized, and the question of the status of people who had never heard the gospel was reopened. Kant's philosophical revolution moved the question of truth from the task of determining objective truth about the world "out there" to the investigation of internal experience, which opened people to the possibility that we might all harbor different truths about the world without the consequence that only one could be right while all the others had to be wrong. This made Schleiermacher's liberalism possible, because he focused on describing individual experience rather than defining dogmatic truth. Throughout the nineteenth century, educated people in the West learned more and more about other religions, and by the end of the century were beginning to encounter people of other faiths. The unexpected resilience of other religions in the face of a surge in Christian missions caused a crisis of confidence, and increased migration and the colonial experience itself brought not just individual representatives of other religions but entire religious communities into the horizons of ordinary Christians. Thus, by the time the Immigration Act of 1965 opened the floodgates of immigration into the United States, along with increased migrations into Europe, the Churches themselves were softening their theological positions. Perhaps in 1897 the bishops of the Anglican Communion could condemn Christian fascination with Buddhism and Hinduism, because most Christians in the West would never actually meet an actual Buddhist or Hindu, but by the late twentieth century, people were living and working alongside entire immigrant communities that brought temples and mosques right into their cities and towns.

My contention here is *not* that external circumstances completely determine theology. If that were true, then in any given time and place, the theology of world religions would be utterly uniform throughout Christendom. Rather, it is that one cannot understand the theology of any Church with regard to other religions without examining the historical and cultural moment to which that theology speaks and which frame its concerns. The history of Christianity's many modes of relationship with other religions is a long one, and—here's the payoff—you, dear reader, are part of that history. As you ponder your own attitude toward other religions, remember that you are just as embedded in a certain cultural setting and historical moment as Jesus, the early Church fathers, the councilors at the Council of Florence, the conveners of the Edinburgh Missionary Conference, or the assembled bishops of the 1988 Lambeth Conference. Attention to your own situation will help you in thinking through your own theology of world religions, because in doing so you will become aware of what you need your theology to do, and with what situations your theology needs to equip you to cope.

With this in mind, we will close our historical survey, and turn our attention to the theological options that form the framework for contemporary discussions of religious diversity in Christian circles.

II

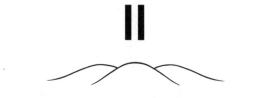

Theological and Practical Elements

Up to this point, we have focused exclusively on the *is* rather than the *ought* of interfaith relationships. Our concern has been to look at what actually has been said and done as Christianity came into contact with other religions, from its inception to the present day. We have seen that theologies do not descend from above to offer pristine and disembodied truths, but are formulated by religious groups as responses to the concrete needs and circumstances of their times. This came out most clearly in the changing theological stances adopted by Church bodies in their official documents, but we also saw it to some extent also in the writings of individual theologians.

But let us be clear about what we are *not* saying. We have not observed that theology follows historical and sociological developments slavishly, as if all one needed to know was the history, social structures, and other elements of a given Christian group in a given time to derive its theological stance. It should be clear that Christians do not move in lockstep with the times or with each other, so what we actually see is a set of theological trends distributed across a spectrum. For example, while we focused on the more open theologies of St. Clement, St. Justin Martyr, and St. Irenaeus in chapter two, we also noted that a number of their contemporaries were perfectly willing to affirm the maxim "outside the Church, no salvation" and consign adherents of other religions to perdition. Within any given historical and sociological context, the interplay between integrity and openness remains active, giving rise to a *range* of responses rather than determining one single response.

In part two we will be examining the theological options that are in play today when Christians think about the status of other religions and try to decide on the proper way of relating to them. Our historical survey has given us insights into the reasons why the questions have arisen in the first place (the apparently permanent presence and resilience of other religions) and why they are framed in certain ways (focusing on the religions themselves rather than on the status of individual non-Christians), but it has hardly led us to a single answer to the questions so raised and framed. In chapter five we will look at the full range of theological reflections on other religions, from the exclusivist to the parallelist, and see the breadth of responses that have been offered within the contemporary context. In chapter six we will first look at the practical approaches that Christians take to other faiths, both in dialogue and evangelization, and then consider the thorny issue of relating these two apparently contradictory approaches to each other.

5

Current Theological Models

In this chapter we will learn about the primary ways in which theologians and philosophers of religion understand religious diversity in relation to Christian truth. The most generally accepted model for classifying theological positions consists of three categories: exclusivism, inclusivism, and pluralism. Though this typology remains in wide use, some scholars question whether the categories adequately cover all possible theological options, and I believe some of the criticisms are valid. I will accordingly modify this scheme in two ways to make it more comprehensive. First, I will divide the category "inclusivism" into two subtypes, which I call the "in spite of" and "by means of" models. Second, I will add another category called "parallelism" to describe a theological position that began to emerge in the 1990s.

As we proceed, I will first present the basic outlines of each of these models and give some examples from past and current theological writings in order to bring out the variations that are possible within each model. Then, after describing the general features of each of these models, I will analyze the advantages and disadvantages of each position.

Exclusivism

Overview. Simply stated, an exclusivist theology of other religions holds that Christianity is correct and alone able to save souls, while other religious traditions are not. Though this statement may appear to be unambiguous and well defined, exclusivists still have room to take different views of the value of other religions. In its *weak* form, exclusivism may hold that only Christianity (or even only one's own subtradition within it) brings about salvation, while still admitting that other religions can have some positive, though non-salvific, benefits. In its *strong* form, it holds that other religions are positively dangerous, and lead only to hell or perdition. This strong form is the more conservative position and is generally associated with fundamentalism, while the weak form has been espoused by some evangelical theologians.[1] Whether strong or weak, however, all these theologies hold that adherents of other faiths are in need of evangelization in order to be saved. They tend to be distrustful of what they regard as a "relativizing" of Christianity as one faith in a peer group of other, equally good faiths (the view that, as we saw earlier, the Roman Catholic Church refers to as indifferentism). They affirm both the uniqueness and the universality of Jesus Christ, the impossibility of salvation outside an encounter with and acceptance of him as one's savior, the authority of the Bible as the final frame of reference in all matters, and the precedence of the missionary imperative over any effort to dialogue with other faiths.

Examples of this theology are certainly not hard to find; some can be found by simply tuning in to the broadcasts of various televangelists. One of the most influential modern statements of this position is the Lausanne Covenant, ratified by participants in the International Congress on World Evangelization held in Lausanne, Switzerland, on July 16–25, 1974. Section three of this covenant, titled "The Uniqueness and Universality of Christ," reads as follows:

> We affirm that there is only one Saviour and only one gospel, although there is a wide diversity of evangelistic approaches. We recognise that everyone has some knowledge of God through his general revelation in nature. But we deny that this

can save, for people suppress the truth by their unrighteous-
ness. We also reject as derogatory to Christ and the gospel
every kind of syncretism and dialogue which implies that
Christ speaks equally through all religions and ideologies.
Jesus Christ, being himself the only God-man, who gave himself as the only ransom for sinners, is the only mediator between God and people. There is no other name by which we
must be saved. All men and women are perishing because of
sin, but God loves everyone, not wishing that any should perish but that all should repent. Yet those who reject Christ re-
pudiate the joy of salvation and condemn themselves to eternal separation from God. To proclaim Jesus as "the Saviour of
the world" is not to affirm that all people are either automatically or ultimately saved, still less to affirm that all religions
offer salvation in Christ. Rather it is to proclaim God's love for
a world of sinners and to invite everyone to respond to him as
Saviour and Lord in the wholehearted personal commitment
of repentance and faith. Jesus Christ has been exalted above
every other name; we long for the day when every knee shall
bow to him and every tongue shall confess him Lord.[2]

It is important to note that the preceding paragraph affirms that
even non-Christians have some knowledge of God, but it rejects any
claim that this natural revelation has any power to save. It also flatly
denies any salvific efficacy to other religions, no matter how otherwise spiritually profound or ethically advanced they may appear, and
no matter how devout and sincere their adherents might be. This is
the essence of the exclusivist stance: There is no other road to salvation except through an explicit acceptance of Jesus Christ as one's
savior. Corollary to this is the consequence, also strongly affirmed
above, that all Christians have a duty to engage the world by proclaiming this truth, and not by holding dialogues with the other
religions.

Christians outside of conservative circles generally appraise this
theological stance quite negatively, and the criticism most frequently
raised is that this position is "intolerant." Here, however, one must
make some careful distinctions before passing judgment. Intolerance is not a characteristic that naturally attaches to any particular

theological position; rather, it is an attitude that persons all across the theological spectrum may display. "Liberals" can be just as intolerant as "conservatives" when they decline to engage perceived adversaries, demonize them, seek to deny them opportunities to express their position, or refuse to have anything to do with them. As we saw in chapter one, some intolerance is unavoidable if any person or group is to maintain a certain level of integrity. One cannot label any theological position intolerant in and of itself. One must first gauge the extent to which proponents of a position are willing to interact with and give credit to the good faith of those who disagree with them.

A good example of a Christian who would be an exclusivist by any measure and yet who exhibited broad tolerance is Karl Ludwig Reichelt, a Norwegian Lutheran missionary to China in the early twentieth century. He went to China to spread the gospel of Jesus Christ, and continued throughout his stay there to believe that Christianity was superior to all other faiths. In the 1920s he resolved to establish a Christian Mission to the Buddhists, with a special emphasis on converting Buddhist monks. Nevertheless, he befriended many Buddhist monks, and became one of their staunchest defenders against the attacks frequently published by his fellow missionaries. Acknowledging that the ranks of Chinese Buddhism included the usual mixture of good and bad, he pleaded for a balanced and informed view and lauded the piety and accomplishments of the more eminent monks of his acquaintance in genuinely warm terms.[3] He was, in short, a tolerant exclusivist.

One element that appears within the weak form of exclusivism, and helps to temper its attitude toward other faiths, is its recognition of their potential role in helping to predispose their adherents to receive the gospel at some later point in their lives. As the extract from the Lausanne Covenant reproduced above indicates, many conservative Christians are able to see and acknowledge natural revelation, which is either a self-revelation of God or a purely rational deduction of God's presence, that human beings can derive from the world around them and which therefore might form an element in their religious beliefs. Beyond natural revelation, God might still communicate directly with human beings to some degree in order to orient them toward the truth and enhance their readiness to receive it. Insofar as other religions help people to restrain their sinful tendencies and teach them to attend to realities larger than themselves and their own agendas and desires, they may indeed play a positive role in preparing them to hear the truth. This concept is often denoted by the Latin phrase *preparatio evangelica*, "preparation for evangelism."

Thus, whereas the strong form of exclusivism regards other faiths as simply deceitful and denies them any positive value, the weak form provides a way to look for God's hand at work within non-Christian communities. Nevertheless, the reader should remember that even the weak form represents an exclusivist position as long as it denies that other religions can ever go beyond merely preparing people for evangelism and bring about their *salvation*.

Evaluation. In evaluating the exclusivist position, we may note that it exhibits several significant strengths. First, it is certainly a logical position, one that is unwilling to affirm that two contradictory claims might both be true "in their own way." This makes it easy to present and explain clearly. This is not always acknowledged as a strength, however. As we saw in chapter three, the Kantian "turn to the subject" as it was refracted through Schleiermacher's *Speeches* gave many Christians a good reason to affirm that two different positions could still be valid, and this view makes claims to complete logical consistency suspect, at least as a criterion for promoting one vision of truth over another. As we shall see, some would argue that this is a disadvantage, not an advantage.

Second, the exclusivist's conviction of the truth of Christianity gives her or him a valuable perspective on other religions. Because they are generally very clear on their own religious commitments and identity, and are not in search of further answers, exclusivists frequently see other religions more clearly and can sometimes listen to and understand them more accurately than proponents of the other theological positions that we will examine shortly. For example, Galen Amstutz has pointed out that historically, three groups of Western-

ers have engaged in the study of Japanese religions: early missionaries, religious seekers, and scholars (who frequently arise from the
ranks of the seekers). Of these three, he found that the missionaries,
in their newsletters and books, frequently saw and described the
Japanese religious scene much better than did the other two groups.
The missionaries, interested mainly in getting to know the competition and living in the field for many years, saw clearly that the Pure
Land School was the largest and most significant of the Buddhist
schools in Japan, while the latter two groups, based on more personal
quests and agendas, gave an unjustified pride of place to Zen.[4]

Despite these strengths, exclusivism presents difficulties as well.
It calls into question God's mercy and good judgment when one
takes into account the millions of human beings who either lived before the time of Christ or who never heard the message of God during any period of history. As we saw in chapter three, it was possible
up until the discovery of the New World to believe that every nation
had already been exposed to the gospel message, and so this problem did not arise. However, after the Age of Discovery, it became
abundantly clear that the world included entire populations that had
not heard the gospel and had died in an ignorance for which they
could not be held responsible. A strict and thoroughgoing exclusivism that makes no provision for the salvation of people who have
never heard of Jesus and never had even the opportunity to convert
runs the risk of making God a capricious and unjust judge who con-
demns people for a lack of faith that is not their fault. This is as true
for the weak form of exclusivism as for the strong form, since both
deny salvation to these populations.

A second disadvantage can come about when an exclusivist fails
to actualize the second strength listed above. Though it may be true
that the clarity and commitment of the exclusivist stance have enabled some to take an objective look at other religions and form a
reliable picture of them, there are others who, because of a preexisting commitment to depicting other religions as false, only attend to
their negative aspects and present them in an unflattering and distorting light. Instead of giving their audiences the kind of balanced

picture of other faiths that Reichelt rendered of Chinese Buddhism, they offer a one-sided, inaccurate portrayal. For example, Kenneth Boa's book *Cults, World Religions, and You* makes a very brief presentation of the form of Hinduism propagated in the 1960s by Ram Dass and dismisses it as nothing more than worship of a statue of a monkey.[5] However one may evaluate the early teachings of Ram Dass, it is a distortion of Hindu belief to omit explaining the meaning of General Hanuman, leader of the monkey army in the Indian national epic *Ramayana*, as a symbol of the perfect devotee of the highest God. When identified and exposed, such misrepresentations of other religions only bring discredit to their perpetrators.

Conclusion. When coupled with a tolerant attitude and an inquiring mind, the exclusivist position offers a theological model of active listening and engagement from a position of deep personal conviction and integrity. Exclusivism names a broader category of religious attitudes than one might expect, and can include elements that range from the severe position that other faiths are evil or delusional, to a more positive position that at least some other faiths—to the extent that they teach selflessness and service and predispose their adherent to attend to the transcendent—might serve as "preparations for the gospel." In no instance, however, does this position in any of its forms ascribe actual salvific value to other faiths. Crossing that line takes one out of the exclusivist camp and into the realm of inclusivism.

Inclusivism

Overview. The inclusivist model of theology differs from the exclusivist chiefly in that it sees a possibility that salvation may be available outside the bounds of the visible Church community. Whereas exclusivism would, as we have seen, deny the possibility that anyone could be saved without explicitly accepting Christian teaching and belonging to the Christian Church, the hallmark of an inclusivist attitude is the proposition that members of other faiths *can* achieve salvation without necessarily converting to Christianity, or indeed without ever having heard the Christian message. Thus, a Buddhist or a Muslim could still, under certain conditions, be saved in the specific way that Christianity defines salvation without first knowing about Jesus Christ or converting to Christianity.

Past presentations of the inclusivist position have conflated two distinct visions regarding what these "certain conditions" for salvation might be, and whether to evaluate the role of non-Christian religious traditions positively or negatively as factors in bringing about salvation for individuals. I find it helpful to break this category down into two subtypes. The more conservative form of inclusivism might be dubbed the "in spite of" model, meaning that if persons of other faiths are saved, their salvation would take place "in spite of" their home tradition. The other model, which we will consider shortly, I have called the "by means of" model, in order to highlight the fact that, according to this way of thinking, God saves people of other faiths "by means of" their own, non-Christian faith traditions.

The "In Spite Of" Model of Inclusivism. This model of inclusivism entails a fairly negative assessment of other faiths. In a sense, this type of inclusivism would agree with the exclusivist model in saying that other faiths constitute obstacles to salvation, but it breaks with exclusivism in not denying the possibility that non-Christians might actually be saved by God's grace. They affirm, however, that salvation, if it comes to the adherents of other religions at all, comes in spite of their religions and, in fact, negates them. A good example of this model is to be found in the *Chronicles of Narnia*, by C. S. Lewis. In the last book in this series, *The Last Battle*, we find a singular character remaining on the battlefield at the conclusion of the final conflict.

To set the scene briefly, the followers of Aslan the lion, the Christ-figure in these novels, are distinguished from the followers of another god called Tash. Tash is depicted as monstrous both in text and illustration, and the teachings of his cult are presented as deceitful and evil. In short, the religion of Tash is simply wrong, and following it accomplishes nothing good; its adherents must convert and leave their former faith and god behind. An apocalyptic final battle takes place between the Calormenes who follow Tash and the Narnians who follow Aslan, and it ends with the victory of Aslan's forces.

So far, this scenario would be compatible with an exclusivist view of things. However, after the battle we find a single surviving Calormene soldier still in the field, whom Aslan approaches. Contrary to the soldier's expectations, Aslan accepts him and, surprisingly, states that the soldier has actually been serving and worshiping him all along. How could this be? the soldier wonders. Aslan explains that even though this soldier *thought* he was worshiping Tash, an examination of the soldier's conception of the character and attributes of his god shows that it corresponded more to Aslan than to Tash, and the way he has conducted his life conforms to Aslan's moral teachings, not Tash's. Consequently, Aslan claims the good deeds the soldier performed during his life as service to him, even though they were done in the name of Tash. In other words, the soldier was quite mistaken in thinking he was worshiping Tash in the first place! In reality he was worshiping and following Aslan, and Aslan finds this acceptable and welcomes the soldier into his flock.[6]

The detail to notice in this literary example is that the *actual* religion of Tash is of no account in making the soldier acceptable to Aslan. If the soldier is "saved," it is *in spite of* his presumed affiliation with the cult of Tash. Assuming that Lewis meant to convey his actual theological stance through this fictional episode, we may follow his lead and conclude that in the real world of multiple religions, a Buddhist might find at the end that she has actually been following the teachings of Jesus under the name *Buddha*. Somehow, God would have broken through the "static" of Buddhism in order to communicate God's own nature, own love, and own commandments to her, even if she had never heard the gospel preached. While agreeing with exclusivism that other religions fundamentally are in error, this kind of inclusivism would still affirm that those of other faiths can be saved by God's own free action, while the exclusivist would deny it.

There is a somewhat more charitable form of this view that is based on the idea of *preparatio evangelica*, which we examined above. Whereas the view described above would see other faiths as simply harmful and wrong (something Lewis stressed by depicting the religion of Tash as evil and Tash himself as a monster), a softer view would affirm that other religions, though not able to save, can still help to prepare their adherents for a future encounter with the gospel. This belief would be consonant with the softer type of exclusivism in asserting that non-Christians can benefit from their religions. However, exclusivists would claim that this benefit does not extend to salvation, at least not until human evangelists arrive and the people actually have a chance to hear and accept the gospel. Inclusivists would break with this view by saying that at least *some* members of other religions are more than just "prepared" for eventual salvation; they actually are saved through God's direct intervention.

Certain documents of the Roman Catholic Church take this position. Many documents authored by Pope John Paul II state that people of other religions may, by God's grace and the working of the Holy Spirit, find salvation. However, the Vatican document *Dominus Iesus* cautions that this does not mean that other religions constitute vehicles for salvation in and of themselves, but are, at best, preparations for the gospel:

> Certainly, the various religious traditions contain and offer religious elements which come from God, and which are part of what "the Spirit brings about in human hearts and in the history of peoples, in cultures, and religions." Indeed, some prayers and rituals of the other religions may assume a role of preparation for the Gospel, in that they are occasions or pedagogical helps in which the human heart is prompted to be open to the action of God. One cannot attribute to these, however, a divine origin or an *ex opere operato* salvific efficacy, which is proper to the Christian sacraments. Furthermore, it cannot be overlooked that other rituals, insofar as they depend on superstitions or other errors (cf. 1 Cor. 10:20–21), constitute an obstacle to salvation.[7]

This document puts forward the clear view that other religions may have elements of grace in them and that specific rituals and teachings of other religions may well constitute vehicles for the Holy Spirit to speak directly to the heart. But in and of themselves, these rituals and teachings are not sufficient for salvation. While this agrees with Lewis's position that the other traditions cannot be the means of salvation, it differs in that it declares that elements of those religions can be the doors through which the Holy Spirit comes into the heart and transforms it, preparing it for salvation; it is difficult to imagine the vicious rites of Tash performing that function.

Although this may represent a higher view of other faiths than the hard version that finds nothing good about them at all, it still maintains the distinction that characterizes the "in spite of" model of inclusivism: *people* of other faiths may be saved by God, but the *faiths themselves* do not save. The only difference between these two constructions of the "in spite of" model stems from the affirmation or denial that the religions themselves play *any* positive role in predisposing people for the inner work of the Holy Spirit. If one asserts that the religions themselves provide the means by which salvation is actually accomplished, then one has crossed into the "by means of" model.

The "By Means Of" Model of Inclusivism. Other inclusivists evaluate non-Christian faiths more positively. They assert that the teachings and practices of other religions, far from constituting mere obstructions that God must overcome to save people, can actually serve as vehicles that carry their adherents to salvation. This eliminates the distinction just mentioned between individuals and the faiths they profess. On this reading people are indeed saved by God alone, but God accomplishes it *through* their faiths. Such considerations came into being when theologians of the late twentieth century began to broach new questions: Could it possibly be that other religions can serve as channels for God's saving activity? Could it be that God's plan of salvation actually included a place for other religions from the beginning? Did God always intend for there to be a multiplicity of faiths?

To give an example from one such theologian, Karl Rahner raised these questions in the 1960s in his *Theological Investigations,* fully aware that many Christians would find these suggestions novel. Nevertheless, he reasoned that if we believe God desires the salvation of all humanity, then God must have made an orientation toward salvation an integral part of human nature. If that is so, then people would be likely to act on this orientation. However, people cannot do so except within their own concrete, particular social and historical circumstances; it is not a grace that comes "out of the blue" and with no relation, or even with an adverse relation, to a people's actual life together (as the "in spite of" model might have it). Thus, in accord with their God-given nature, people will spontaneously create social structures that express this basic orientation, and God makes use of these structures as channels to reach out to them. The most obvious places to look for these concrete channels for God's saving grace are within the religions themselves as the structures through which people most intentionally turn to the divine. Rahner saw in other religions an expression of God's love for all humankind and an outworking of humanity's inbuilt desire to turn toward and seek God. By the sincere practice of their religions, other people could come to full salvation; Rahner called such people "anonymous Christians." If, at some point in their lives, they were to hear the gospel, they would recognize in it the basic orientation of their lives as already lived, and accepting it would be like coming home.

I should make clear that Rahner strongly affirmed that God saved all humankind by means of Christ, but not necessarily by means of "Christianity." However, he was cautious not to appear to be downplaying the importance of Christianity or of the Church. He was quite explicit in his affirmation that salvation, even if medi-ated by other religions, was a means of grace that God had prepared for those who, through no fault of their own, had not heard the gospel. Once the gospel had been presented, those who rejected it bore the responsibility for their choice. Nevertheless, in Rahner we have a clear example of the "by means of" model of inclusivism—those of other faiths can be saved by God working through their re-ligions rather than in spite of them.

Other theologians, following this lead, have advocated a move away from "ecclesiocentrism," by which they mean an excessive focus on the visible structures and boundaries of the Church itself, and to-ward other focal points: "Christocentrism," a focus on Jesus Christ as the mediator of salvation, or "theocentrism," a focus on God's saving acts in human history. Their point is that God's endeavors to save all humanity reach beyond the bounds of the Church, and that Christians should be open to the possibility that God, operating freely, has saved others whom they might not recognize as Christians. Also, whereas Rahner was seeking to solve the specific problem that arose during the Age of Discovery, namely, the problem of God's relation to those who had never heard the gospel through no fault of their own, many Christians today affirm a broader form of "by means of" inclusivism, believing that adherents of other religions who practice sincerely may be saved by God working through their home traditions *even if* they have heard and declined the gospel of Jesus.

Evaluation. As should be clear, both models of inclusivism share one defining feature: the affirmation that people outside the Church who have made no explicit conversion to Christianity might still be saved through God's free grace. It must be noted, however, that the salvation is still a specifically *Christian* salvation. The practices of those outside the Church may have been directed toward rebirth in the heaven of Vishnu or the attainment of Paradise or eternal release from suffering, but in the afterlife they will find themselves at the wedding feast of the Lamb. What are the advantages and disadvantages of such a position?

The most obvious strength of this position is that it overcomes the primary weakness of the exclusivist stance. As seen above, exclusivism has difficulty accounting for the fates of people who, due to circumstances beyond their control and for which they can take no responsibility, have not heard the gospel preached. As long as a strict exclusivism holds that salvation cannot occur without an explicit acceptance of Jesus, such people are condemned, even if common sense must judge them innocent and their condemnation unfair. Inclusivism opens the door for God to act in God's own way to rectify the situation. This position allows for the possibility that God can, through God's own free and merciful action, make a way for those who have lived their lives beyond the reach of missionaries, evangelists, and preachers to enter God's kingdom outside of the "normal channels" of conversion and Church membership. This position thus satisfies our basic intuition that God must be both merciful and just.

The next factor to which we call attention might be taken as either an advantage or a disadvantage, depending on one's theological orientation. Inclusivism appears to call into question the necessity of missions, particularly the call to proclaim the gospel. While some inclusivists such as Rahner are careful to affirm that Christian proclamation is still necessary in order to bring the "anonymous Christian" to full self-awareness and to bring the Good News to all others, it is still easy to make the leap to thinking that people of other faiths are all right just as they are, particularly within the framework of the "by means of" position. Rather than evangelize others, many proponents of both the inclusivist and pluralist positions (to which we will come next) believe that *dialogue* is a more appropriate means of interreligious interaction; by opening channels of communication between religious communities, we will come to know and celebrate the many ways in which God has worked throughout human history to bring all to salvation.

A third perceived strength is that the inclusivist view promotes a more open and tolerant attitude toward other faith communities, something that is indispensable within a society marked by religious diversity in which a wide variety of people need to get along if it is to function. Many Christians believe that inclusivism is more likely to foster an attitude of openness and listening, whereas the exclusivist stance appears to encourage a closed-mindedness and judgmental attitudes. However, I hope I have shown in the section on exclusivism that *any* theological position can exhibit either tolerance or intolerance. Thus, we must critically re-examine the assumption that this advantage automatically attaches to inclusivism and not to exclusivism.

A fourth advantage is that inclusivism encourages Christians to look for the good in others and acknowledge it when it is found. People of all faiths who live in religiously diverse societies, such as the United States or India, are exposed to members of other faith communities every day, and they often note the piety, sincerity, and moral seriousness of other people. In the face of this, it becomes hard to believe that God would consign clearly good and decent people to eternal perdition, and the inclusivist stance enables those persons to see a way in which God can also honor genuine goodness and holiness. Thus, inclusivism seems to corroborate their experience of others and enable them to live together more peacefully.

We must note some problematic aspects of inclusivism, some of which call the supposed advantages of the position into question. First, although it is generally felt that inclusivism makes for a more open attitude toward other religions, we find that it paradoxically can impede genuine understanding. To give an example, when I was in Taiwan researching Chinese Buddhism there, I presented the idea of inclusivism to some of my Buddhist friends, and was surprised when they informed me that they found the idea offensive. They told me that if I really thought *my* God was saving *them* through their Buddhism, then I had obviously not been listening to them. They were Buddhists; they did not believe in God. Their practices were aimed at gaining liberation from an endless round of suffering and rebirth, not entrance into heaven. They did not believe human beings even had a soul to be saved, and so on. In contradiction to what many inclusivists believe, it appears that exclusivists, who are not committed beforehand to finding their own faith reflected in the beliefs and practices of others, are able to hear and understand the actual content of other religions better than inclusivists! This problem will surface again when we consider the pluralist position.

Second, the "by means of" model of inclusivism, especially in its more theocentric form, calls into question the necessity of Christ's suffering, death, and Resurrection. If it is true that one may be saved by means of Buddhism, then why was Jesus' suffering and premature death necessary? The Buddha lived to be eighty years old, and spent the last forty-five years of his life quietly teaching the people. If this is efficacious for salvation, then why would Jesus need to undergo torture and death? Inclusivist theologians today are noticing this qualm, and some, like Jacques Dupuis, answer the objection in this way: Though it may be true that Buddhism sometimes serves as a vehicle for salvation for those Buddhists who have never heard the gospel, it remains true that the salvation Buddhism mediates to its followers comes about only through Jesus' death and Resurrection.

In other words, Jesus' saving action remains central to making salvation possible, no matter through what channel that salvation might come to any given individual.

Inclusivism is a popular stance among many Christians today. Its affirmation of the primacy of God's love toward all seems to encourage a kinder attitude toward others, its openness to other faiths appeals to those who must live with believers of other religions in their daily lives, and its encouragement of dialogue between faiths widens and enriches the Christian's view of the world. Nevertheless, the fact that inclusivism still privileges Christianity as the "most correct" or "most adequate" religion troubles some theologians who wonder if God, the cosmos, and reality itself can be adequately encompassed by *any* human religious tradition. We will examine their alternative next.

Pluralism

Overview. Is it possible for any one religious tradition to have complete and exhaustive access to truth in a way that is denied to other traditions? Or is reality something so great that any single person or community can only catch glimpses of it and apprehend certain aspects of it while the whole of it remains mysterious? The pluralist position would answer no to the first question, and yes to the second. A pluralist theology denies primacy to any one religious tradition as either "the only true religion" or "the most true religion." To illustrate this, many employ the following ancient Indian parable, which many readers will no doubt find familiar.

One day, four blind men encountered an elephant. One reached out and touched the elephant's ear, another its side, another its leg, and the last took hold of its tail. The first declared, "This thing is very much like a snake." The second said, "No, it is more like a palm leaf. How could you think this is like a snake?" The third scoffed, "You're both wrong! It is like a wall." The fourth countered, "You are all crazy! It is like a rope with a frayed end." And so the four blind men argued, and even came to blows, each one claiming to know the true nature of the elephant and convinced that his three companions were wrong.

This story has a certain appeal, and the fact that it has been told and retold for thousands of years and crossed many cultural boundaries indicates that it expresses a nearly universal perception of the limitations of human knowledge. Indeed, it is hard to disagree with the proposition that, when faced with the cosmos in all its vastness and mystery, human beings are like the blind men. We can grasp only part of it, we can see it only from a certain subjective angle, and no one can claim to have the whole truth. Pluralism asserts that the religious traditions face these limitations as well. As human communities, none of them can credibly claim to have the entire truth in a way that no other does. While an inclusivist theology places Christianity at the center and sees other religions as incomplete or deficient versions of it, pluralism places reality itself at the center, and claims that *all* religions, even the pluralist's own, are incomplete and subjective, and grasp only fragments of the whole picture.

Not surprisingly, many religions acknowledge that there are constraints on our innate abilities to know, but then claim to be exempt from them, either (1) by declaring that *their* own truths originate from a source outside the human community not bound by human limitations, or (2) by maintaining that their founders, though coming from within the human community, achieved mental states that enabled them to pass beyond the normal limits. The first strategy claims *revelation*; the second claims *enlightenment*. As examples of the first claim, Christianity, Judaism, and Islam say that their basic truths are not human discoveries, but revelations from God. Because God is the omniscient creator, God's knowledge is not subjective and fragmentary, but objective and complete, and therefore by attending to God's revelation, human beings can get the full picture of their situation and path. In China, Daoists came to claim that their primal sage, Laozi, was himself an embodiment of the principles that organize all reality, and thus his message also comes from outside the purely human realm, from reality itself. The second type of claim may be found in traditional Hinduism, which states that the texts of the Vedas were first perceived by seven legendary seers whose religious practices gave them access to knowledge beyond that available to ordinary human consciousness. Similarly,

Buddhism and Jainism teach that their truths were discovered by enlightened men who achieved omniscience by means of their spiritual self-cultivation. Whichever argument they utilize, the world religions all ground their doctrines and practices in a credible knower who has access to and bestows wisdom that is unavailable to the rest of humanity. Indeed, the claim that truth breaks in from outside the human domain is the essence of religion, according to the definition adopted in chapter one.

Pluralism, however, does not agree that the extraordinary origins that certain religions claim for their teachings give them an exemption from its critique. *Even if the stories are correct*, they affect only those who attained supernatural knowledge or received revelations. The rest of humanity, including the overwhelming majority of religious people, may claim no such privileged knowledge. The reception of revelation or enlightened teaching, whether it comes from reading the Bible or chanting the Rig-Veda, becomes an ordinary act of human knowing, subject to the same limitations outlined above, always partial and always perceived from a certain angle. Christians who are familiar with the history of biblical interpretation know that even their divinely revealed texts have been understood within concrete Christian communities in an astonishing variety of ways that seem dependent on such factors as language, history, and local culture.

The pluralist argument is, at its base, a plea for humility in the face of the final mystery of reality, and a hunch that other religions, coming at the world from other perspectives, might see things that we do not. To a certain extent, a great number of people in modern religious communities would agree that our ability to apprehend reality has limits and that there are mysteries beyond our ken that other religions might be in a better position to see. At times this humility is coupled with the view that the great sages and mystics of all religions, those who give their followers revelations, had essentially the same vision of ultimate reality, but had to communicate it to their (unenlightened) followers in the particular language and concepts of their own place and time. A popular image for communicating this view envisions all religions as paths leading up different sides of a mountain, but all terminating at its peak. This is the "common core" theory of religious diversity: a revelation of one and the same truth is at the core of every religion, and the great teachers of history point their followers to it, but from different directions depending on their starting point. Though followers of the religions may not know this core teaching or the final goal it points to at present, it will all become clear once we have arrived.

Some pluralist thinkers go beyond this, however, and try to see what this mystery might be that can be seen in so many different ways. No thinker is more well-known in this regard than John Hick. As one might critically examine the accounts given by all the blind men in an effort to reconstruct the elephant, Hick has spent several decades sifting through the data of the world's religions in an attempt to synthesize the reality of which they all present a piece. His thought is quite subtle, and a real understanding of it requires a much deeper presentation of both Western and Eastern modes of thought than is possible here. In brief, Hick has proposed that all religions point to a quality that he calls "the Real." Furthermore, the Real is compelling—knowledge of it elicits not just recognition and assent, but a moral response as well. In pointing people to the Real, religions also push them to transcend their own self-centeredness in order to make them Reality-centered. In other words, seeing "the big picture" necessitates seeing one's own finite place within it, and that in turn prompts one to move beyond one's purely personal concerns and to integrate one's actions and desires into the world at large.

According to Hick, the ultimate truths articulated by the many religions all derive from an apprehension of this single Real. Even forms of ultimate reality as diverse as the single and transcendent God of Judaism and Islam, the trinitarian and incarnational God of Christianity, the impersonal Brahman underlying all phenomena in Hinduism, and the patterns governing reality that constitute the Dao in Daoism—all point to the Real, which is truthfully (though only partially) described by all of them and yet goes beyond any of them. Similarly, the ethics taught by all religions, as diverse as they are, serve the single purpose of enabling individuals to rise above their own narrow desires to pursue a greater good in harmony with other people and with the natural world.[8]

Evaluation. The pluralist position has obvious strengths. It agrees well with most people's understanding of their own limitations. Few people would claim to know and understand everything, and few who make this claim gain credence. It is natural for us to think that our minds have limits to what we can know and process, and in many spheres outside religion, we are well aware that we can benefit enormously from listening to others and trying to see things from their various angles. If the blind men would stop arguing and compare their notes on the elephant, they might well arrive at a far more accurate and complete picture of it than any of them could gain on their own; why should it not be so among human religious communities?

Also, in a religiously diverse society, such a view seems to provide a common ground for people of different faiths to meet and engage with one another. The inclusivist view privileges one's home tradition and leads to a distortion of the other's religion as a result of the effort to see it as an extension of one's own, and it sometimes gives offense to others on that account. The pluralist view, by contrast, seems to require no such preconceptions and lessens the risk of offense. One is free to enter into dialogue with the other to see what Reality looks like from another perspective. That seems to lead to a more open and authentic dialogue than one might have from a starting point of inclusivism.

Nevertheless, the pluralist position brings problems of its own, the first of which qualifies the second of the position's strengths that we have just discussed. Pluralism is indeed more likely than inclusivism to provide a way of approaching other religions openly and learning about them without prejudice, but it turns out that it still runs the risk of distorting them to some degree because of its assumptions. The urge to see some deeper underlying Reality reflected in other religions can blind the pluralist to the very real divergences that come forward when one attends to the particular teachings that define the religions. If one presupposes that all religions point to the same Reality, then genuine contradiction cannot be recognized because it is assumed that it cannot arise. For example, it tends to skirt the very real difference between Christianity, which teaches that one must have faith in God to be saved, and Buddhism, which teaches that belief in a creator deity that will save one is an obstacle to liberation. The rush to find common ground affords little motivation to notice differences, and it is in the differences that religions claim their real significance and identity. For most Christians of a pluralist persuasion, this problem goes unnoticed due to simple ignorance of the details of what other religions actually have to say. If one does not know the Buddhist teaching regarding the harm of believing in creator deities, it becomes much easier to assume that Buddhism and Christianity point in the same general direction.

The problem here is that ignorance leaves a vacuum in our knowledge of others, and that vacuum is too easily filled by projection. Several years ago, some members of my parish went to hear the Dalai Lama speak in Washington, D.C. They brought back a copy of the benediction he had used to end his talk, and my Christian friends were taken with the beauty of the text. They brought it back to church and asked that it be used in the liturgy during a Sunday service. When I saw the text, I was shocked; how could this Buddhist blessing possibly fit into a Christian service? After a moment's thought, it occurred to me that as a specialist in Buddhist studies, I knew the concepts on which the text was based and the technical meanings of its words, while my fellow parishioners did not. That made it all too easy for them to read Christian meanings into it, and then rush to celebrate the "common" teachings and goals that Christianity and Buddhism shared. In this case, genuine study and dialogue would have been quite useful in advancing mutual understanding, but it would not necessarily have led to the conclusion that Buddhism and Christianity point to the same teachings and goals at all.

However, many theologians who have adopted the pluralist position *are* quite knowledgeable about the real differences between faiths, and attempt to account for them in their writings. This effort leads to the second main problem with pluralism: the attempt to fashion a model of the Real that transcends all apparent divergences in belief and practice leads to nothing more than a religion composed of the broadest and most banal commonalities. For instance, Hick and his followers have been chided for the "bleaching out" effect of their analysis. Critics charge that once all the differences have been removed and one has distilled a set of basic truths that accord with the teachings of *all* religions while contradicting none, what remains is thin and bland. To say that all religions point to the Real and that they function to make people Reality-centered is to say very little. With everything that is distinctive about the religions bracketed out, the residue, however harmonious, proves abstract and remarkably free of content or interest.

The third criticism of the pluralist position comes from a more philosophical angle. The evangelical theologian S. Mark Heim has argued that, logically speaking, a pluralist position simply is not possible. On the one hand, the basis of pluralism is the belief that the cosmos, the Real, the ultimate, the absolute, is beyond human knowing, whether the "knower" is a single individual or a large religious community. What can be known, then, is only a part of the whole seen from particular subjective angles. On the other hand, however, this claim that all are partial views of *one and the same* reality depends on some person or community getting beyond those limitations. The only way we know that the blind men are all handling various parts of the elephant is that *we are not blind and can see the whole elephant*; the only way to know that all religions are different paths up the same mountain is that *we can stand at the top of the mountain and see all the paths converging there.* For Hick to make credible his claim that all religions point to a single reality (the Real), he would have to have a privileged point of view above and beyond that of the religious communities themselves.

According to Heim, that is a contradiction within the very premises of pluralism. If human beings, as individuals and communities, are by nature limited in their abilities to know reality, then the pluralist has no more claim to know "the way things are" than does any other person or group. Thus, far from inhabiting a platform above all other religions from which their common referent can be seen, pluralism stands on exactly the same ground, becoming one more religious view among others. Furthermore, inasmuch as pluralists confront members of other religious communities and inform them that what they believe as their own distinctive religion is actually an instantiation of the pluralist worldview, pluralism becomes another form of *inclusivism*, and not *pluralism* at all.[9] Remember that inclusivists hold their own religious worldview to be the most adequate, and if people of other faiths find salvation, that salvation is made possible in terms of the inclusivist's home tradition. The pluralist is saying that people of all other religions will be saved through means discerned by pluralists (they will achieve "Reality-centeredness" in Hick's terms) and will come to a realization of truth as defined by pluralists (Hick's "the Real" rather than God, Krishna, or anything else).

This seems to be a fairly devastating critique, but it only applies when the pluralist goes beyond noting the limitations of human knowing and tries to define more precisely what it is that the religions only know in part. That we humans can know only so much is a commonsense observation with which few would disagree. It strains logic, however, to reason from that simple observation the conclusion that all the religions, insofar as they try to discover and illuminate the truth, must be pointing to the same thing. My own observation over the years is that Heim is quite correct in pointing out that the pluralist position ought to be viewed as a religion in its own right. In most conversations I have had with ordinary "people in the pews," the pluralist option functions as a religious belief, a starting assumption, a way of looking at the data of religion, and a tool for interpreting that data; it does *not* generally come about as a result of long and detailed examination of the actual beliefs of other religions. Those who assert that all great mystics have had the same basic experience of truth prove, when asked, to know very little, if anything at all, about what Meister Eckhart, Teresa of Ávila, Dogen Zenji, Muhammad, or the Buddha actually said of their experiences. Such an examination, when carried out, reveals stark and irreconcilable differences, even between the various mystics and enlightened masters.[10]

Even those who have made such an investigation and claim to have verified the common referent of all religions become suspect after some thought. In the nineteenth century, the Indian mystic Sri Ramakrishna claimed to have tried the spiritual practices of many different religions and carried them through to their successful conclusion. He thus claimed to have proven through his own experience that they all led to the same reality. However, it is quite possible that the reason the results were so similar was not that the reality to which the practices led was the same, but that it was the same person carrying them out. One may still question whether Ramakrishna actually replicated the experience of another or saw exactly the same truth.

So far, the only theological option that has maintained an ability to look at other religions objectively and describe them in a way that reflects their real distinctiveness and character is exclusivism. Yet many Christians are uncomfortable with the exclusivist's conviction that he or she has grasped the whole truth (or at least enough of it to bring about salvation), and the assertion that all other religions are fatally wrong. Is there some way to maintain the strengths of all the above positions while avoiding their weaknesses? Can we continue to affirm the good we have found in our own home tradition, acknowledge the obvious limitations of human knowing that call for humility, honor the perception of genuine "elements of grace" that can be seen in those of other faiths, and continue to believe that God loves and desires the salvation of all people, all the while maintaining the exclusivist's ability to hear what the other religions have to say about what they teach and value? The attempt to bring all these factors together has led in recent decades to the emergence of another theological option.

Parallelism

Overview. The parallelist position is perhaps the most difficult to explain and defend philosophically. In an attempt to maintain all the strengths listed above while avoiding the pitfalls of other positions, contemporary theologians such as Heim and the Roman Catholic scholar Joseph A. DiNoia have proposed a new paradigm that puts religions on parallel tracks. Rather than saying that they all lead to the same goal, whether it be the Christian goal (as the inclusivist would affirm) or some reality that is beyond any particular community's understanding (as the pluralist would maintain), the parallelist position holds that all religions are *not* the same, that their particular teachings hold true in an important sense. When the Buddhists say that there is no creator God and that the best thing for humans to do is to break the bonds of endless rebirth in the bliss of nirvana, we should assume that they mean exactly what they say, and that they are serious about it. When Christians assert that the primary human problem is alienation from God and that our goal should be to attain heaven by claiming the reconciliation brought about by Jesus' death and Resurrection, we should assume that they also mean what they say, and that they are equally serious about it.

So far, an exclusivist would agree. Parallelism breaks with exclusivism, however, in refusing to say that one or the other is simply wrong, affirming rather that both are correct. Buddhist beliefs and practices will lead to Buddhist-defined goals, not to hell. Christian beliefs and practices will lead to Christian-defined goals. Muslims who are serious will attain Paradise, and committed and sincere Vaishnava Hindus will attain the realm of Vishnu outside the ordinary world of suffering and endless reincarnation. The philosophical difficulty that this position poses should now be quite evident. Parallelism appears to assert a *plurality of absolutes*.

Is this possible? How are we to understand this?

S. Mark Heim, in his book *Salvations* (note the plural), makes use of a philosophical concept called "orientational pluralism" to describe what this might mean. As a way into his presentation, let us draw an illustration from language. Let us imagine that two people, both native English speakers, come upon an object. One of them remarks, "That's a very nice sofa." The other one responds, "That's not a sofa; that's a bench." They then proceed to have a tedious argument about what the object ought to be called, a sofa or a bench, and each might appeal to other people to support their opinions. Now let us make one crucial change in the scenario. The two people are no longer both English speakers; one speaks English, the other Chinese. As these two people come upon another object, the English-speaker says, "That's a very nice table." The other, once this statement has been translated for him, responds in slow and heavily accented English, "That is not a table; that is a *zhuozi*" (Chinese for "table"). They too proceed to have a long and tedious argument about whether this object is properly called a table or a *zhuozi*.

The first argument may strike one as rather silly, but one might still see that it has a point to it. Many readers may feel that if they could just see the item under discussion, they too would have an opinion as to whether it is a sofa or a bench. As members of the English-speaking community, we do have to come to some agreement on the proper usage of words if we are to communicate with one another at all. The second argument, by contrast, has no real point at all. The reader does not even need to see what the object of their argument looks like because the object itself is not the issue. In the second case, the argument is between members of two different language communities who are both perfectly correct about their assertions *within their own communities of discourse*. For an English speaker, *table* is the correct word to use; for a speaker of Mandarin Chinese, *zhuozi* is equally correct. The first argument is meaningful because it is between two members of the same community of discourse; the second is meaningless because it cuts across the boundaries of two such communities. Depending on the community to which one belongs, one or the other word may be correct *for that community*, but there is no way to judge which word is correct in any absolute sense.

This is still a little too simplistic to do justice to Heim's theory, so let us complicate the case a little. Table and *zhuozi*, though different words, at least point to the same sort of thing-in-the-world. Not all words in other languages have exact counterparts in English, however, and sometimes a more fundamental disconnect arises. Take, for example, the Chinese word *shaonian*. As a student I learned that it meant "youth," and so when I encountered it in Chinese literature, I read it as meaning essentially what the English word *youth* meant.

Once I arrived in Taiwan and began studying Buddhist organizations, though, I found to my surprise that groups I understood to be youth auxiliaries included members up to forty years old; how could they be youth groups, then? Only after much time had passed did the thought occur to me that the Chinese did not invent the term *shaonian* just to translate the English word *youth*. It was a native term that had its own range of meaning for speakers of Chinese, independently of any proposed English translation equivalent. *Shaonian* simply meant anyone between about twenty and forty, and that was that. Under these circumstances, we see that the two language groups do not merely utilize different words for the same thing; they go further and divide reality into different "parcels," and *then* they name those parcels. Beneath the words lurk different conceptions of what constitute the very things to be named. An argument about the words *youth* and *shaonian*, therefore, would involve more than a simple disagreement over what word to use to name a group of people; it would be a disagreement over the actual constitution of the group to be named. Again, there is no right or wrong here; whether you group together people between the teen years and the late twenties, or between the twenties and the late thirties, each may be entirely correct for each linguistic and cultural community.

This is the essence of orientational pluralism. Religions, like languages, are communities of discourse, and each community puts together the pieces of reality in its own way in order to construct its own web of observations, meanings, and actions that make sense within that community, but which have no way of gaining meaning within the web constructed by another community. A Christian may say that God exists, loves all humanity equally, and has provided the means for their salvation, while a Buddhist may deny the existence of God, and say instead that people are trapped within an endless round of rebirth that entails only suffering and calls for practices such as meditation and compassionate action in order to gain liberation. To say that one is right and the other is wrong is as pointless as arguing whether a given object with a flat surface and four legs ought to be called a table or a *zhuozi*, or whether the terms *youth* and *shaonian* ought to cover the same periods of people's lives. There may indeed be an object or a group of people out there that calls for us to name it, but the radically different linguistic and conceptual structures within which it is named have no point of contact, and no argument is possible between them. Similarly, says Heim, there may indeed be a reality out there,[11] but we can approach it only as members of communities who come at it from within long-established systems of meaning that provide no basis for an argument over who is right and who is wrong. The reader would be correct to hear in this Kant's "turn to the subject."

When we encounter the variety of religions, each assessing the human condition in different ways and prescribing different routes to its final fulfillment, we are not simply dealing with varying sets of propositions that may be taken at face value and judged more or less adequate. Behind each religious doctrine is a whole complex of values, attitudes, cultures, languages, and any number of other elements; many of them will reside in the deep background, and the religious person may not even be aware of them. These constitute the "orientation" out of which religions come, and their assertions and recommendations for practice can be understood only within the framework of that orientation. What is more, while competing doctrines and practices arising within a given orientation may be reconciled or combined within the framework of that orientation, the conflict between orientations themselves cannot be. A given person or group can have only one orientation at a time, just as a person can speak only one language at a time; an orientation that might hypothetically arise from a deep engagement with the Christian and Buddhist frameworks and bring them together is no longer either a Christian or a Buddhist orientation; it is something else, something new, and other Christians and Buddhists may not be able to accept it as something they can recognize from their own orientations (the analogy from language would be with creole or pidgin that combine elements of two languages into something new). The teachings of each religion, therefore, are not to be reconciled by saying that one is right and the others wrong (exclusivism), or by saying that one is more right and the others partially right (inclusivism), or that *all* are only partially right (pluralism). They each stand as independent communities of discourse that approach reality through structures of meaning and action that have internal coherence, but cannot be set alongside one another for comparison or adjudication. All are completely right *in their own terms.*

But does this mean that, as we asked at the outset, there is a plurality of absolutes? Can they all be right about reality when they say such vastly different things about the world and society we live in and the human condition we inherit? Heim deals with this by separating the question of understanding ultimate reality from that of salvation within the world's religions. Religions are not just statements about reality as such; they are recommendations for action in order to attain a goal of some sort, and the goal is the "salvation" sought by adherents. In most cases, attainment of the goal does not require understanding ultimate reality; indeed, many religions say that the final nature of things is beyond the human ability to know: whatever is ultimate, be it Reality itself or God, is ineffable and mysterious. Indeed, Christians generally agree that God is ultimately unknowable in an exhaustive way, but that people *can* know just what they need to be saved: that Christ died and rose again for our sins. The level of knowledge needed to attain salvation is far from absolute knowledge about the final nature of things, and that being the case, it is possible to imagine that many religions could posit many different courses of action for different ends, and that all of them can work. The Christian, praying to and trusting in God, can experience a Christian salvation. A Hindu can practice devotion to a form of God and experience the end of the endless merry-go-round of reincarnation.

Thus, in Heim's presentation, one can still affirm that there is only one reality rather than a multitude of absolutes. However, our *experience* of this reality can vary widely, as can our response to that experience. In the end, the salvations advocated by different religions are experiences, each sought and valued from within those religions' orientations, and each attained in a real sense.[12]

Evaluation. The strength of this position arises from the fact that it overcomes the weaknesses of all the previous positions. Unlike exclusivism, it does not call one immediately to declare any religion wrong that does not agree with one's own, and does not condemn people unfairly for not following a path of which they were innocently unaware. Unlike inclusivism and pluralism, it provides a rationale for one to listen carefully to what other religions say about themselves and understand them in their own terms without "shoehorning" them into preconceived ideas of what they *ought* to be and say. Unlike pluralism, it does not reduce all religions to their most general common elements, arriving at an abstract and banal version of truth barren of all that is distinctive and compelling about the religions of the world. Finally, it corroborates what scholars and specialists in comparative religion often find, namely that the religions, when studied in depth, really do reveal differences in outlook and practice so radical and fundamental that it seems that a dialogue would indeed be a dialogue between two incommensurable orientations.

Still, parallelism brings problems of its own. At least in Heim's formulation, it relies on the kind of intellectual trend that we noted in chapter three: the "turn to the subject" and a focus on the world as experienced rather than on the world as such. Heim's parallelism depends on the assumption that salvation is essentially an experience a person has within a particular orientation that is embedded in various social, economic, historical, cultural, and linguistic contexts. Only by understanding all these background factors can one really understand why any given person would construe the world in such a way that they would come to believe in a certain kind of salvation and formulate a specific set of practices to attain it. (This even omits to notice the fact that many religions do not believe there is some overall problem with the human condition that requires anything resembling salvation at all.) Some readers may sympathize with Samuel Johnson, who, on hearing the idealistic theories of Bishop Berkeley, kicked a stone and declared, "Thus I refute Berkeley." In other words, many religious people believe, and quite seriously too, that their religion has a great deal to say about reality-as-it-is, and that certain actions such as kicking stones will have effects that do not depend on one's beliefs about what *ought* to happen. Just as kicking the stone will hurt one's foot, practicing anything other than Christianity and not putting your whole trust in God *will* produce an undesirable outcome regardless of one's orientation.

So, one may question whether the notion of orientational pluralism, drawn from philosophy, can be appropriately applied to religion. The theory is persuasive only if one accepts the premise that no person can transcend their particular "orientation." Though this may be true of other areas of inquiry such as philosophy, economics, and politics, the reader should remember that religion is different. Recall that, in chapter one, we defined religion as the frame of mind that draws its view of reality and its motivations for action from beyond the human realm. Whether religious truths are said to come from divine revelation or human enlightenment, what makes them "religious" is precisely the claim that they transcend the human condition and its limitations in some way. Most religions that aim their followers toward some form of salvation base their practices on a view of the world that comes from somewhere above the human realm. A few, such as certain forms of Buddhism, Hinduism, and Taoism, actually predicate their salvations on the achievement of a transcendent insight that takes the practitioner beyond human limitations, beyond *all* orientations. Thus, religious people may find it difficult to go along with Heim's separation of the questions of absolute truth from those concerning practices leading to salvation. It may seem that if religion is simply an orientation to reality, then it isn't really "religion" at all.

Further, one may wonder whether parallelism really deals with any of the questions raised by religious diversity, or merely moves them to another level. Whether one posits a diversity of religions or of orientations, one still has diversity and one still must deal with it. In addition, Heim's assertion that orientations are incommensurable, while it may be perfectly true, seems to make the prospect for real, productive dialogue much more difficult. Mutual understanding begins to look less like dialogue and more like learning another language so as to be able to translate. Many who have engaged in dialogue report that it is very much like that, and so perhaps Heim's presentation could serve to alert us to the real depth of the problems that arise in interreligious encounter. It certainly allows us to look at the problems of religious diversity from a compelling new angle.

All that being said, the idea of "orientations" may be a useful one for many purposes. It does seem to describe with accuracy the perception many have that a particular dialogue partner comes into the conversation with such a different set of core values and assumptions that a great deal of spadework will be necessary to uncover them before real communication is possible. It may be too that "orientations" do not line up with what we consider "religions." Even within a single Church body, such as the Episcopal Church, one finds that conversation between people of "liberal" and "conservative" inclination looks much like what Heim describes as the encounter of different orientations. Even if "orientation" does not cover the same range of meaning as "religion," we might still have a use for a term that describes the fundamental ways in which people experience, process, and respond to the world as they find it.

Conclusions

Where does this leave us? While the four positions examined above appear to cover all the religious options (leaving out the *nonreligious* options of dismissing all religions as wrong, or as mere psychological coping strategies or social constructs), none of them appears to offer a clear solution with no attendant difficulties or unintended consequences. Thus, one must choose one's theology with the understanding that all the alternatives have both strengths and weaknesses.

What have the Churches themselves done, and what positions have they taken? Among Christian ecclesial bodies, the majority of those who have produced official statements have opted for either exclusivism or inclusivism (the latter sometimes awkwardly conflating both of inclusivism's subtypes). The reason for this is not difficult to see. To be religious is to have a view of the world; it is to believe something to be the truth. Both exclusivism and inclusivism share the property of allowing, even requiring, believers to maintain their doctrines in a serious way. Exclusivism enables Christians to take the totality of their beliefs as clearly reflective of ultimate reality, and brooks no logical contradiction; if other faiths have other things to say, they are simply wrong. Inclusivism permits some flexibility around the edges, and holds open the possibility that individuals outside the Christian faith, or even other religions as such, may get at least the crucial things right. Other faiths may even be effective paths to salvation, but in the end, the Christian description of God, the world, and the human situation is the right one, and if other faiths embody some level of truth, it is only insofar as their teachings reflect Christian beliefs and encourage Christian practices, or only insofar as God exercises grace freely to save whom God wills.

For some Christian groups, such as Unitarians and more liberal subgroups within other denominations, the visions of pluralism and parallelism may be more compelling. For Christian individuals and groups who put less store in formal doctrines, who value diversity, and who wish to be more realistic about the limitations of human knowledge, the latter two positions will be appealing in that they give weight to the active role that people play in constructing their own realities and affirm that, through dialogue, we can multiply our perspectives and, in learning to see things from multiple vantage points, enrich our lives tremendously.

6

Balancing Dialogue and Mission

(In chapter four we looked at the history of missions in the late nineteenth and early twentieth centuries, and we saw that a conflict developed between those who saw evangelism as the only proper way to relate to other religions and those who began to see dialogue as an alternative. Both activities are carried on with great enthusiasm today, and the tension between proponents of one or the other certainly continues unabated. In this chapter we will look at some contemporary ways of going about dialogue and missions, and then we will examine ways to lessen the tension between them. Finally, we will see that too much focus on the mission-dialogue dichotomy keeps us from seeing the wider picture in interfaith relations.

Ways of Doing Dialogue

Studies of interreligious dialogue that have been undertaken to date generally follow the analysis put forward in the Roman Catholic document *Dialogue and Proclamation*,[1] which states that four main types of exchange take place in the modern world: (1) Theological or philosophical dialogue takes place when representative intellectuals of the religious traditions meet to exchange and compare doctrines and ideas. (2) In contemplative or monastic dialogue, practitioners of spiritual disciplines such as meditation or prayer gather to compare experiences rather than ideas. (3) Social welfare dialogue is more of a cooperative venture in which members of various religious traditions engage together in activities that accord with shared values. (4) The "dialogue of life" is a more informal and spontaneous form of dialogue that appears when people of various faiths live or work together and engage in the give-and-take of common life. Over the last few years, I have noticed another form of dialogue that seems to have escaped the eye of observers up until now: (5) In the dialogue of art and culture, people of different communities share the artistic and cultural expressions of their faiths. We will have a quick look at each of these in turn, and see some examples of these differing forms of dialogue in action.

Theological and Philosophical Dialogue. Theological and philosophical dialogues are perhaps the least accessible form of dialogue for the average believer, as they tend to involve professional, working Christian theologians and academics, along with their counterparts from other faith traditions. In this type of encounter, scholars and thinkers gather to compare and discuss the finer points of their intellectual traditions, and the conversation generally proceeds in fairly abstract theoretical terms. A good example of this sort of dialogue is a series of conferences involving Buddhists and Christians that began in the early 1980s under the encouragement of the Protestant theologian John B. Cobb, Jr., and the Japanese Zen scholar Masao Abe. These dialogues, which today go by the name "Buddhist-Christian International Theological Encounters," convened off and on for over twenty years, and came to involve a growing number of thinkers from wider segments of the Christian and Buddhist communities. The topics considered and compared in these encounters have included Buddhist and Christian ideas of ultimate reality and the nature of the human condition. These interchanges led to the establishment of an academic organization, the Society for Buddhist-Christian Studies, and a journal, also called *Buddhist-Christian Studies*, which comes out annually.

To the average person, such exchanges may seem rather dry, and the results each side achieves would not appear to extend beyond simply accumulating data on the other. Some participants, however, have explored the possibility of entering deeply into the other's religion, developing an understanding of the other side that might be close to an "insider's" view. The theory presented by the theologian John B. Cobb, Jr., for example, recommends something he calls "crossing over and crossing back." That is to say, the Christian in dialogue must listen and hear the other to the extent that she or he learns the religious "language" of the other and can use it fluently. Just as people learning a foreign language might go and live abroad for a time and immerse themselves in the language by using it to the exclusion of their mother tongue, so religious persons in dialogue can immerse themselves in the idiom of their partner religions until they "get it" at the most profound level. Christians so engaged are not to cease being Christians, but are to return to the Christian community, made fit by their experiences to serve as bridges to or interpreters of other religions. Following the analogy with language, one might say such a person has learned the speech of the other to the point of "near-native proficiency," but without losing his or her own native language in the process.

The Buddhist-Christian encounter is far from being an isolated example. During the same time frame, a set of scholars mainly based in Boston has been conducting a series of Confucian-Christian dialogues on topics of social ethics and the foundation of morals. Muslim-Christian-Jewish dialogues have also been held in the Washington, D.C., area to compare ideas regarding prophecy, scripture, and the bases of social institutions among the three monotheistic faiths. Although the ostensible goal of such dialogues is better mutual understanding of the intellectual aspects of religious traditions, an interesting side effect of these encounters has been a kind of cross-fertilization. Many Christian theologians have begun to incorporate what they have learned from dialogue partners and sent theology in some new directions. This is the genesis of the "comparative theology" of which I spoke in chapter four.

Contemplative-Monastic-Spiritual Dialogue. While theologians and intellectuals meet to discuss ideas, contemplatives meet to compare experiences. Among Christians, one finds this sort of dialogue occurring almost exclusively among Churches that have monastic institutions, in particular Roman Catholics, Eastern Orthodox, and Anglicans. This kind of dialogue may take place in individual monasteries and convents, where representatives of the contemplative branches of other traditions are invited to come and talk about their experience of either meditation or prayer. Muslims from the Sufi orders, Buddhists, and Hindus have participated in these sometimes ad hoc events. A more formal expression of this form of dialogue can be found in the Monastic Interreligious Dialogue (MID), founded by the Benedictine Confederation in 1978. This organization of Benedictines and Cistercians has its own activities apart from the intellectual engagements going on elsewhere. The MID has held two significant Buddhist-Christian Monastic Encounters at the Trappist monastery of Gethsemani in Kentucky, Thomas Merton's home, and these dialogues have produced wonderful volumes of essays from participants.

As with the intellectual dialogues described above, the contemplative encounter with other religions has also brought about some new developments in theory and practice. At one level, familiarity with other religious practices and experiences has led Christian participants in these exchanges to understand their own experiences with prayer in new ways. Thus, the May 2004 issue of the *Monastic Interreligious Dialogue Bulletin* observed: "Over the past 25 years we have learned from happy experience that monastic interreligious dialogue, while increasing our understanding and appreciation of other religious traditions, also helps us come to a deeper comprehension and a fuller expression of our own spiritual and theological heritage."[2] At another level, this spiritual exchange, like the intellectual exchange, has led to some cross-pollination as Christian contemplatives have learned the practices of other traditions and incorporated them into their Christian practice, most notably adapting Zen meditation as a way of quieting the soul before God. This interchange has been so lively that some Catholic priests and nuns have received formal Zen training and have been certified as Zen teachers by Japanese masters. One may now find books that use the spiritual practices of Asian religions in Christian contexts.[3]

Social Welfare Concerns and Activism. Virtually all the world's great religions include teachings on social justice along with their theologies and their contemplative practices, and frequently the social values put forward bear enough commonality with one another to make cooperative ventures in social welfare work possible. Buddhists, Muslims, Jews, and Christians all have teachings on the necessity of charitable giving and work on behalf of the poor, for example, and while the theological teachings that undergird these activities may vary, the actual hands-on work that they encourage may be very similar or even identical. As an example of this sort of cooperation, we may look at an agency here in my own hometown, the InterFaith Conference of Metropolitan Washington (IFC). This is an organization that has, since 1979, brought together Christians, Mormons, Buddhists, Jews, Sikhs, Jains, Zoroastrians, and Muslims not only for dialogue but also for common welfare work. The IFC helped to establish an interreligious food bank, and is currently engaged in environmental work and child advocacy, among many other projects. People affiliated with the IFC have brought together youth and leaders from the various faith communities around Washington, D.C., to build a house through Habitat for Humanity. The "dialogue" occurs in the common effort expended, and in the informal conversations on the job and during breaks.

There is a gray area between this sort of dialogue and the more intellectually oriented dialogues that we looked at first, and that is the area within which formal roundtables convene to discuss social action and justice issues from the perspectives of the faith traditions. For example, the International Buddhist-Christian Theological Encounters that we discussed previously went more in this direction during the 1990s. Having looked earlier at more purely theoretical issues, they began considering these two religions' teachings concerning women's issues, environmental issues, globalization, and so on. Some of the Muslim-Christian-Jewish trilaterals organized through the Catholic University of America School of Religious Studies also involved explorations of practical social problems in addition to abstract theoretical issues.

The "Dialogue of Life." The fourth major area of interreligious dialogue identified in current scholarship is the vast and informal area called the "dialogue of life." While all three forms of dialogue that we have examined so far take place at determined times and places and through planned activities, the dialogue of life occurs spontaneously whenever people of different faiths live and work together. It consists of the ordinary, day-to-day interactions that take place over the fence, around the coffeepot, during meetings, or in the innumerable other venues of common life. In a very real sense, this is a dialogue that does not need to be planned and coordinated; it is the flow of conversation that just happens whenever people live with one another.

In a way, this is the most important dialogue of all. No matter whether one's basic intention in interreligious encounter is dialogue or evangelism, one must build on relationships worked out in ordinary social interactions to produce any kind of significant results. Daily social life is the arena within which we build these relationships. Over the last several years, I have had Muslim colleagues and graduate students, and as we have gotten to know one another as friends and fellow workers over time, we have come to like and trust one another. With a warm and friendly relationship already established, I know I can go to them with questions about Islam and enjoy free and frank exchanges of views. The same applies to my relationships with the rabbis and Jewish students I've worked with over my career. I have many Chinese Buddhist friends both in the United States and Taiwan. I first made contact with them in connection with my formal studies, but after many years of working, eating, and singing together (mostly karaoke), we have a solid relationship that enables me to tackle the most difficult interreligious questions with them.

Thus, even though the dialogue of life may not look like real interreligious dialogue as it proceeds in casual conversations and greetings in the home, school, and workplace, it is the indispensable foundation we must lay if any of the other forums for dialogue are to function effectively. Beyond facilitating more formal events, though, this natural and spontaneous dialogue can do best one of the functions that all have agreed dialogue should perform: help to avert conflict and establish peace among the religions. A good example of this was seen after the terrorist attacks of September 11, 2001. In the days and weeks that followed, many Muslims in America (and even people who were mistaken for Muslims) came under attack and many properties were vandalized. During this bleak time, many people came to the defense of the U.S. Muslim community because they had lived and worked alongside Muslims for many years and knew that they had to protect their friends. When someone lobbed a rock through the front window of an Islamic bookstore in Alexandria, Virginia, the town Chamber of Commerce came forward with a check to repair the damage, because the bookstore had been a good member of the business community for many years. Instances such as this can show us the healing power of the dialogue of life.

Cultural and Artistic Dialogue. One of the most memorable events of my professional life took place in March 2002. The government of Saudi Arabia invited me and the dean of my school to come to the capital city of Riyadh to participate in a conference called "Islam and the Dialogue of Civilizations," and we were joined there by delegates from around the world. Most were Muslims from various places—the Middle East, Indonesia, Malaysia, North Africa, the United States, even Japan—along with non-Muslim leaders and academics. We had presentations on a number of topics having to do with the relationship of Islam to the non-Islamic world. To look at the heavy schedule of speakers and the titles of their presentations, it would have appeared that this was primarily a dialogue of the first type, intellectual and theological, with some discussion of historical and political issues as well. However, other elements were to be found around the edges of the event.

In a gallery attached to the main venue, we were told, there was a display of Qur'anic calligraphy, and we were heartily invited to take it in. Islam has historically enforced the divine injunction against making images of any living creature or natural object, and so has little real representational art, but calligraphy, especially the decorative inscribing of words from the Qur'an, was encouraged as an acceptable form of artistic expression. In addition to this visual art, during one of the plenary sessions, a delegate from England named Yusuf Islam—the former pop star known as Cat Stevens— interrupted his talk on the cultural activities he is currently pursuing to chant some verses from the Qur'an. Such chanting has also been a valued art form in the Islamic world. Both the calligraphy and the chanting served to show the non-Muslim delegates the Muslim sense of the beauty of the divine word, and brought out a sense of the sacredness of the Qur'an as it is specifically seen in Islam, in a way that a purely academic lecture could never have conveyed.

Another example of this cultural and artistic dialogue may be seen in the annual interfaith concert organized by the InterFaith Conference. This event, which always draws hundreds of listeners, brings together Jewish cantors, Muslim imams who chant Qur'anic verses, African American gospel choirs, Protestant Church choirs, the local Sikh chorus, Catholic choirs and monastic chanters, and others in a celebration of religious music from all faiths. This event is more "dialogical" in that, unlike an exhibition of the artistic products of one faith, it gathers people to share their art with one another in a free exchange. Like the exhibition described above, it represents a chance for members of one religion to share with those from another not just what they believe or what they've experienced, but what they find beautiful, uplifting, inspiring, and nourishing to the soul.

One last example will show how artistic expression may be used not just to share the beauty already to be found within a religious tradition, but to communicate its attitude and approach to other religions. In September 2003 I went to Bangalore, India, to participate in a consultation of NIFCON, the Anglican Consultative Council's Network for InterFaith Concerns. Though much of our time was spent in talking and praying together, we also were treated to several artistic displays, notably an exhibition of Indian Christian paintings at the conference site, as well as a field trip to an *ashram* run by a local Christian painter and sculptor.[4] However, the event I have in mind here is not the gallery display or the trip to the *ashram*, but a dance recital given us by the Christian classical dance troupe Nritya-vani. Two of the three dances on their program depicted purely Christian themes, but the last selection, titled "Jesus and Major Asian Religions," took on the ambitious task of dancing the entire life of Jesus. After the Resurrection, however, the dance went on, and the young woman dancing the part of Jesus embarked on a tour of the Asian religious traditions. She encountered a Muslim at prayer, a Hindu expressing devotion, and a Buddhist at his meditations, and after observing each of them for a time, she smiled and nodded to the audience in approval. In this way the predominantly Roman Catholic dance company expressed its own theology of world religions in the idiom of Indian classical dance.

Some Observations on Dialogue. Over the past fifteen years, I have participated in interreligious dialogues as both delegate and observer, primarily with Buddhists and Muslims, occasionally with Jews. During this time I have made a few observations that may, at first, appear counterintuitive. For the most part, those who go in for interreligious dialogue form a self-selected group. This certainly is good in a way, as it ensures that those who participate in interfaith encounters will be those who feel genuinely called to it. However, it presents some problems as well. The first is that it encourages a premature rush to find common ground, and the second is that it lessens the impact of dialogue on the Churches themselves. Let me say more about these problems, beginning with the search for common ground.

What could possibly be wrong with seeking common ground in dialogue? After all, we are all human, and so we cannot be so very different from one another. If we are to learn to live together, we must begin by finding commonalities so that we start with points of agreement, right? Well, to a certain extent, yes. However, the urge to find commonalities often does not advance the dialogue to the degree that participants hope. If one remembers what was said in chapter one about the "marketplace of religions," the reason for this becomes apparent. In any market, products compete primarily with other products that are trying to occupy the same market niche. Coca-Cola does not compete mainly with Chrysler; it competes with Pepsi-Cola. Why? Because Pepsi is closest to it and competes for the same customer base. The competition between Islam and Christianity is very intense these days, because, among other factors, these two religions are both ethical monotheisms. They compete *because* of their common ground. Thus, in my experience, Muslim-Christian dialogue is very contentious, while Buddhist-Christian dialogue is much more irenic. Buddhism and Christianity are so different that common ground is hard to find, and it is *for this very reason* that they do not compete as intensively. In fact, as we saw in the section on contemplative-monastic dialogue, some Christians put aspects of Buddhism into their Christian practice; it is much more difficult to find anyone who could claim to practice Islam and Christianity simultaneously. Their very similarity has the effect of forcing a choice for one or the other. The upshot is that finding a lot of common ground may actually increase interreligious tension, not ameliorate it.

This may seem negative, but there is a more positive reason for not looking exclusively for commonalities. Certainly we all share a common humanity; if we did not, there could be no dialogue at all. But what we find most interesting about one another in general is not our commonalities but our differences. If I were to get to know you as a person, our common humanity might provide a good basis for our incipient relationship, but I would not want to go on always affirming that we both have two arms and two eyes, stand erect, and speak the same language. What I ultimately will want to explore with you are the very things that make us distinct from one another, because that is what makes us interesting. If you completely mirrored me, I would not need to get to know you at all. Thus, Muslims and Christians in dialogue tend to affirm over and over again that they worship the same God, but at some point they need to discuss the fact that Christians believe in a trinitarian, incarnational God, while Muslims do not. If they do not want to face those differences, then why go to dialogue?

The second problem is that of impact. As I noted above, most participants in interreligious dialogue are self-selected and operate autonomously. That is particularly true of Protestant participants. Though this autonomy gives them a great amount of freedom to explore the possibilities of dialogue without constraint, it also poses a danger. As Harvey Cox pointed out many years ago in the introduction to his book *Many Mansions*, the danger is that those in dialogue with other religions will fail to look over their shoulders from time to time to see if their own home traditions are paying attention or supporting their efforts.[5] Although they may be taking dramatic strides, they may be taking them alone or with only a small group. The Roman Catholic Church has taken a different approach. Though many Catholic theologians certainly do interfaith work on their own, the Church has set up its own Pontifical Council for Interreligious Dialogue in the Vatican, and the United States Conference of Catholic Bishops has its own Secretariat for Ecumenical and Interreligious Affairs. Those who work in the offices are, in effect, "ambassadors with portfolio," and though they may sometimes chafe at the Church's insistence that they be accountable to it, it does ensure that their work will have significance in their Church's life.

Ways of Doing Mission

As we saw in chapter four, the way in which Christians go about missions has evolved along with the development of dialogue through the twentieth century. Throughout most of the history of the Church, those who have sought to spread the gospel throughout the world in response to the Great Commission have taken public and private proclamation as their primary mode. Whether it was Peter's public speech on the first Pentecost (Acts 2:14–42) or Philip's more private encounter with the Ethiopian eunuch (Acts 8:26–40), the examples found in the Bible modeled and encouraged this kind of verbal witness, with the expectation that conversion and baptism would result, and missionaries followed these examples and anticipated the same results. Within Roman Catholic history, the goal was always to convert people and incorporate them into the Church as the Body of Christ, and in the Protestant missions of the nineteenth and twentieth centuries, preachers sought to bring about a personal profession of faith in Christ, leaving the business of joining a Church body for later. In all cases, the light had to overcome the darkness, and words were the matches that would light the lamp.

The missions movement of the nineteenth and early twentieth centuries gathered steam quickly, as we have seen, and many took to the overseas mission fields to proclaim the gospel and win souls for Christ. They enjoyed many successes, and we should never lose sight of the fact that the indigenized Churches that have grown up in Asia and Africa are today very grateful for the work of these evangelists who left home and family behind to travel to all parts of the world, often at great cost and great risk. Many went back home after a few years with broken health, and others died of illness or were killed in the field. Nevertheless, many factors led to a deep reconsideration of the missionary task as the twentieth century progressed. Christians became more aware, for instance, that colonialism was inextricably linked with the missionaries' ability to enter into foreign lands, and that the power imbalances that gave them this access bred resentment among local populations, a resentment that still lingers in many places. Stories of missionary hubris now embarrass many Christians. Holmes Welch tells of a missionary in China named George Smith who entered a Buddhist temple, walked up to the altar, and poked at the images of various gods with his umbrella to make the point that they were lifeless and impotent; he was not much bothered when a few of them toppled and broke, but seized the opportunity to preach an impassioned sermon to the gathering crowd.[6]

Finally, because the state of our knowledge about other religions is so much greater than in those days, and because of the influx of other religions into formerly Christian lands, Christians are not as likely to be dismissive of other religions as "pure heathenism" as they were before. In our day, when one may go and see the Dalai Lama speak in major European and American cities, where Catholic priests may also be Zen masters, and where the shelves of bookstores groan under the weight of books about non-Christian religions for general readers, it is far easier to see the depth and value of other faiths, and far harder to assert categorically that Buddhism, Hinduism, Islam, and the rest must one day vanish from Earth so that all may be Christian. Embarrassment over past missionary tactics, increased sensitivities to local religious sentiment, loss of political power in foreign territories, and heightened knowledge of other religions has called forth some new models of mission. We can briefly describe two of them here: one that I call the "Buddhist model," and another that I will call the "leavening model."

The "Buddhist" Model. Many Christians are not aware that before the twentieth century, only three religions ever sent out missionaries: Buddhism first, followed by Christianity and Islam. Twenty-five centuries ago, the Buddha sent his own followers out to preach his *dharma* (teachings) in the towns and cities of northern India and beyond, much as Jesus sent forth the seventy disciples. However, the Buddha gave his followers specific instructions on how to preach the message: Go into a new region and simply settle down among its people, learn their language, and become part of their life. Above all, do *not* preach the *dharma* unless you are explicitly invited to do so. To this day it remains the custom for a Buddhist preacher to refrain from speaking until someone asks her or him to present the teachings, and even when a lecture has been advertised for weeks in advance and the audience is present and ready to listen, the lecturer will not start until a delegation from the audience comes forward and formally requests teaching.

Today, many Christians, even if they know nothing of Buddhist history, are looking at this sort of a model as an alternative to the traditional method of going into a new area and beginning right away talking to and preaching at perfect strangers. This is a way that allows the "dialogue of life" to lay the groundwork of building relationships of trust before presenting the Christian message. Thus, many recent missionaries to foreign countries, especially those that harbor suspicion of Christians' motives and methods, have adopted a strategy much like the ancient Buddhist techniques to present Christ. They do not go abroad as "missionaries," but as workers in other fields, such as health, public sanitation, or civil engineering. They live among the local population and learn their language, customs, and religious practices. They wait for the time to ripen to bring up the subject of religion, either when someone specifically asks them about their faith or when they see an opening in the dialogue with their hosts in which they might graciously bring it up without alienating people who, ideally, have become friends.

This is certainly an improvement over the more extreme scenes of the past, when missionaries, backed by colonial offices and military garrisons, could leap onto the altar at a temple during a festival and harangue the crowds or topple images to the ground and break them. It allows a gentler space within which relationships can build, it encourages the missionaries to listen and learn in a spirit of dialogue before they ever present the gospel, and, in politically sensitive situations, it is the most prudent way to proceed. However, it continues the goals of the past in that it still aims at making a verbal presentation of the gospel that is intended to persuade others to convert to Christianity. The next model questions that goal in a more radical way.

The "Leavening" Model. Remember that in chapter four I recounted the story of how the Taiwanese Buddhist nun Zhengyan founded the Tzu Chi Compassion Relief Association in the 1960s: One day Zhengyan was visited by three Catholic nuns who tried to convert her to Christianity, partly by pointing out that Christianity showed a much greater level of social compassion than Buddhism at that time, building hospitals and orphanages and taking care of the downtrodden. Zhengyan, it will be recalled, did not embrace Christianity, but rather responded by founding a Buddhist charitable organization. In chapter four I presented this story as an example of the way other religions resisted the incursions of Christianity by taking what they saw as its strengths, incorporating them into their own religious practices, and then interpreting them in their own religion's terms. Thus, in this instance a Buddhist nun adopted what she saw as one of Christianity's attractions in Taiwan (strong social welfare programs), brought it into her own Buddhist practice, and provided a specifically Buddhist understanding of it. In this way she resisted the gospel, and the nuns who came to see her that day in 1966 probably regarded the encounter as a failed attempt at evangelism.

However, new thinkers in missions like Douglas Horton (1891–1968), president and general minister of the Congregational Christian Churches and primary founder of the United Church of Christ, might see the same episode differently. In his view the nuns were in fact quite successful, because they communicated one of the core values of Christianity into another religious tradition very effectively. Or, in the language of *Dialogue and Proclamation*,[7] the three Catholic nuns challenged Buddhism through the presentation of "gospel values" and brought about a profound change in Buddhism itself; as a direct result of Christian witness, there is now a multibillion dollar Buddhist charity at work in East Asia that was not there before. Though no one actually converted to Christianity as such, and while the existence of such an organization fills a niche that Christianity might otherwise fill, no one could say that the witness of these Christian nuns was of no effect! In this view Christianity, in this and other cases, provided a leaven that pervaded the host society and instilled the core values of Christianity into it; we should take this as a perfectly valid outcome to a missionary endeavor.

These are two possible compromise positions between the extremes of maintaining the nineteenth-century model of proclaiming Jesus to one and all without necessarily forming relationships on the one hand, and completely abdicating missions on the other. One can, of course, find theologians and missiologists all along the spectrum between these extremes, and perhaps others who might feel that all these options should be left open, and that the real challenge is to discern when one or the other method is the best for a particular situation. But any procedure for evangelization must, in this modern world, be balanced with the necessity of dialogue, and must itself be conducted in a spirit of dialogue.

Tension Between Proclamation and Dialogue: Going Beyond the Dichotomy

Now that we have seen various models of both dialogue and evangelization in some detail, let us revisit the tension between the two, and see if we can get any greater depth of analysis.

Toward the end of our historical survey, I brought up the growth of tension between those who called for increased dialogue with members of other religions, and those who insisted that Christians continue to proclaim the Good News as their primary way of interacting with non-Christians. This tension is not a relic of the last century; it is still alive and well today, and I have experienced it in my own religious work. Within the Episcopal Diocese of Washington, I have been active in both missionary and interfaith organizations. At one time I was a member of a mission support network called Companions in World Missions. At the same time, I was a member of the diocesan Commission on Ecumenical and Interfaith Ministries. I can still recall how, within a two-week period, a member of each group asked me to set members of the other group straight, either by telling those committed to missions and evangelism to leave other religions alone and jump instead into dialogue, or by telling those committed to dialogue to get busy proclaiming the gospel. In this section we will explore the conflict in more detail and see if we can find a way to ease it somewhat.

At the core of the conflict is a sharp divergence in presuppositions about the legitimate purpose of any interreligious encounter. One side asserts strongly that evangelism and proclamation, which aim explicitly at inviting others into Christianity, ought to be the normal motivation for any meeting with members of other faiths. The other side counters that the world today needs dialogue between religions in order to foster peaceful relations and to join forces against irreligion. This divergence is the basis upon which Leonard Swidler, an early pioneer in Buddhist-Christian dialogue, distinguished interreligious dialogue from previous forms of interreligious encounter. The latter, based strictly on assumptions of Christian superiority, led Christians to identify "convert-making" as the primary objective of encounter.[8] One may speculate that in the unlikely event that the "soul-winners" were 100 percent successful, and all the non-Christians became Christians, then the dialogue would collapse for lack of a non-Christian partner.

The primary bone of contention in the debates has to do with

Christians attempting to convert non-Christians, but there is another possibility that some thinkers in interfaith dialogue have raised: the prospect that the other side might convert the Christians away from their Christianity. Some of those who have engaged in dialogue state that for the dialogue to be genuine and sincere, the participants must be truly open to hearing the message of the other side and internalizing it at the deepest levels. These authors see a participant's willingness to enter dialogue with an openness to conversion as a courageous attitude, one that denotes a full commitment to following the lead of truth wherever it may go. Although I am personally aware of only a handful of instances in which this actually happened among Christian participants in dialogue,[9] it seems important to some thinkers that those going into dialogue be aware of that possibility and assent to it beforehand.

Nevertheless, these authors would still affirm that the Christian going into dialogue should never consciously intend to proclaim the gospel to the other side for the purpose of proselytizing. This qualm is partly driven by history. Christianity has always been a missionary religion, and as we saw in chapter four, from the time of St. Peter and St. Paul, evangelists have gone forth into the world proclaiming the Good News and calling people to repent and surrender their lives to Christ. In recent history, Christian missionaries took advantage of the dominance of Western military and commercial power to go into areas of the world already claimed by other religions. British colonial control of India opened the subcontinent to missionaries, the "unequal treaties" with China allowed them access to the Chinese hinterlands, and French colonial rule in Vietnam brought French Catholic missionaries there from the eighteenth century onward. Sometimes cooperation with civil authorities went further than simply allowing unimpeded access: During the seventeenth century, the Dutch authorities that controlled Taiwan punished any display of non-Christian religious practice and exiled the female shamans that had been the religious leaders in precolonial times.[10] The enduring weight of all this history means that, today, when Christians invite members of other religions to the table for dialogue (and the invitation almost always comes from the Christian side), there is some justifiable suspicion that the "dialogue" will devolve into another occasion for seeking conversions. An explicit repudiation of such intentions in advance is sometimes necessary if dialogue is to happen at all.

Given all this, we can understand why a tension exists between the partisans of evangelism and the partisans of dialogue, but is such tension inevitable and must it be permanent? Or is there a way to get beyond it? I think there is, and as a way of opening up some new possibilities, let me tell you about two encounters with fellow Christians that made a deep impression on me.

One day, while I was still pursuing my graduate studies at the University of Virginia, an evangelist appeared on campus. This was not unusual; every once in a while, preachers came to the university to address the students, whom they apparently considered in particular need of the gospel. However, this man was different in his approach from any evangelist I had ever seen before. He stood on a small rise of ground on one side of the main quad (called The Lawn), held an almost life-sized wooden cross in one arm, and harangued the passersby in an utterly impersonal way. He made no eye contact with anyone. When a student approached him, either to argue back or simply to ask a few polite questions, he set his jaw firmly, closed his mouth, and looked away to one side. He refused to talk directly *to* anyone; he would only talk *at* them. In retrospect, he seems to me to represent an extreme case of proclamation with no dialogue.

Many years later, at the conference on Christianity and religious diversity that I attended in Bangalore, I met an Anglican bishop from a small Asian nation who told me that the time for evangelism in his country was over. He said his country had enough Christians already to provide a solid leaven for society, and the proper mode for the future was to engage in interfaith dialogue exclusively. His blunt rejection of the task of evangelism strikes me as representing the opposite extreme, that of dialogue without any proclamation whatsoever.

To see whether the options of evangelization and dialogue are really mutually exclusive, let us ask ourselves whether we need necessarily to follow the example of one or the other of these two men. If we sincerely hold to an exclusivist theology, such as that articulated by the Lausanne Covenant, and believe that all humankind must hear the gospel, would we still want to be like the campus preacher and do so with no element of dialogue at all, no development of personal relationships (or even mere eye contact) with those to whom we preach? On the other hand, if we are more pluralistic or parallelistic in our theology, should we follow the lead of the Asian bishop and state categorically that we will never, ever try to share our faith persuasively with anyone in the future? I suspect that most (though perhaps not all) readers would be uncomfortable if such a choice were demanded of them. The real issue, then, is not which of the two options to choose and which to reject, but how to balance the two, and how to discern the appropriate times and places for each.

Missionaries who do long-term evangelism cannot help but build personal relationships with the people among whom they live, particularly if they remain at their posts for extended periods of years or decades and get to know the local language. If we remember the example of the Norwegian missionary Karl Reichelt, whom we met in the previous chapter, we see that he met with local Buddhist figures at his post in China, and he presented the gospel as compellingly as he could. Sometimes he had success in guiding people to Christianity, but most of the time he received a polite but firm refusal. But here is the crucial fact: After each such refusal, he proceeded to cultivate relationships and enjoyed long friendships with some very influential local Buddhist abbots. He went every week for tea with one to whom he grew especially close, enjoyed many years of dialogue, and learned a great deal about Chinese Buddhism at the same time. We also saw in chapter four that the missionary E. J. Eitel, while so committed to evangelism that he refused to endorse the World's Parliament of Religions, still made a serious study of Buddhism and produced the first western dictionary of Chinese Buddhist terms. These and other missionaries provide a model of genuine and warm engagement even as they pursued their evangelistic task. It was simply not their way to respond to those who rejected their message by snubbing them and moving on to the next "target."

As for the other extreme, the abdication of all evangelism in the pursuit of dialogue, we find here a somewhat trickier case. As stated above, it is a real problem that when Christians issue an invitation to dialogue, those who receive the invitation, remembering the history of Christian missions, quite understandably wonder if the proposed event has evangelism as a hidden agenda. An advance promise not to proselytize may well help a dialogue with new partners to get under way by easing suspicions. This being said, we must also remember that engaging in dialogue means sharing what is most precious to us, and once trust has been established, it is difficult *not* to share with dialogue partners what one finds most compelling, inspiring, and faith-producing about one's own religion.[11] Handled carefully, such honesty is often appreciated. In conversations with Muslims, I have been asked why Christians believe in the Trinity, why we pray as we do, and why we believe so firmly that Jesus Christ is the Son of God. I found that when the dialogue partner sincerely wants to know such things, they expect me to give a full and frank answer and not try to gloss over real disagreements. Such testimonials about personal faith arouse resentment only when they come unasked-for and accompanied by threats, with no willingness to listen to the other side in true dialogue, and especially when the evangelist enjoys some advantage due to political circumstances such as colonial domination. Buddhists in Taiwan resented Christian missionaries in the 1950s and 1960s not because they were preaching their message, but because the funds that they brought into the local economy caused the government to give them unfair advantages in order to keep the cash flowing. Once this changed and the dialogue partners became more equal, things went much more smoothly.

Another argument against completely renouncing evangelism is that not all encounters are interfaith encounters and not all evangelism is aimed at people with preexisting religious commitments. As missionaries in mainland China are finding now, many people in this world are simply lost and in search of direction and healing. Such people may well need the message of salvation in Christ, and to present them with the Good News is entirely appropriate and does not involve proselytizing them away from another religion. However, even in those instances, the would-be evangelist must bear in mind that in today's world, evangelization is rarely, if ever, a simple exchange between two people; it almost always takes place within wider social, political, economic, cultural, and religious contexts, and many people and groups claim a legitimate interest in it. For example, many countries and ethnic groups today understand their recent history as one of humiliation by Western powers (I have heard this claim in India, China, and the Middle East), and large groups, such as the BJP Hindu party in India, are trying to reclaim their religious heritage as part of a wider campaign to regain dignity and a sense of pride in their own culture. Even when preaching to the truly lost, there is a risk of running afoul of larger interests and sensibilities. This means that even an evangelical encounter with an individual who has no strong religious affiliation, however needful, must also contain an element of dialogue, not only with that person but with their local context.

What we ultimately need, then, is not an argument for choosing dialogue over evangelism or vice versa, but a model for relating the two that takes into account their mutual interdependence. If we go back for a moment to the two extreme models, that of the campus evangelist and the Asian bishop, we see that the problem with both of these is that neither leads to any kind of dialogue at all, but each models *monologue* that differs only in the direction in which the monologue flows. The campus preacher wanted a monologue in which only the Christian side speaks, while the bishop projected a monologue in which only the non-Christian side speaks. Any model for interaction that steers between these two extremes will allow for voices to go both ways to create a connection and a conversation between the participants. Once this happens, then regardless of whether the event is defined beforehand as evangelism or dialogue, it becomes a true dialogue. It takes on a life of its own, and moves beyond the predefined agendas to chart new territory.

Let us consult the sociologists. We noted above in chapter two

that early Christianity grew at a remarkable rate: Rodney Stark esti-
mates that it expanded at a rate of 40 percent per decade, so that what
began on the first Pentecost as a movement with three thousand adherents came to number 2.5 million after 250 years.[12] How did this
happen? Stark, in studying modern movements that show similar
growth rates (the Latter-day Saints and the Unification Church) notes
that they grow primarily along the lines of pre-existing social networks. In other words, simply standing on street corners and preaching your message to a crowd of strangers does not work very well;
while you may get a handful of converts and claim some success, it
will not yield the 40 percent per decade rates of early Christianity.
What *does* work is to share your faith with those in your family, among
your friends, and with colleagues and coworkers. Because you already
have a standing relationship with them, they will trust your intentions
toward them; they will be more likely to assume that you are giving
them something you genuinely believe is to their benefit, and that you
are not trying to bilk them out of some money or put more notches
in your belt to bolster your reputation as a "soul-winner."

Although Stark wrote mostly about the phenomenon of conversion, this observation has implications for dialogue as well. As I
mentioned before, even invitations to dialogue, when given to
strangers, tend to elicit suspicion at first. In my own experience,
many formal dialogue events involve representatives of faith traditions who have met for the first time at that event. The result of this
meeting of strangers is not always satisfactory. One hears the same
set speeches over and over, and no real progress is made. In contrast,
the best dialogues I have ever experienced have been with people of
other religions that I have come to know as friends, such as fellow
faculty members at my university or people I have come to know by
working together behind the scenes for dialogue. I will always remember with great fondness a free-wheeling and vigorous discussion I had about Islam and Christianity with the director of a local
Islamic institute while he was giving me a ride in his car. The point is
that both dialogue and evangelism require the building of relationships if they are to be successful, because both are, at bottom, acts of

sharing. Evangelism and dialogue both work best when they are transactions between people who have already become friends; only then can the invitations, either to share our faith or to merely talk together about what we believe most deeply, be given without guile and accepted without suspicion.

There is no need to assume that evangelism and dialogue are so antithetical that the embrace of one requires the repudiation of the other. Some people will always need the message of Christianity, and for them evangelism is a fitting approach. On the other hand, the history of world religions gives little reason to think that the present situation of religious diversity is going to give way to a monolithically Christian world in any imaginable future. Like the poor, other religions are always with us, and unless we intend to cut them off and have nothing at all to do with them, we will always have to maintain mechanisms for fostering dialogue. But even though we can discern between situations where one approach or the other is appropriate, we still see that they interpenetrate so that evangelism is always dialogical, and dialogue, if it shares any honest faith at all, is always witness. It is never either-or; it is always both-and. The real choice we must make is between dialogue and monologue.

The Catholic document *Dialogue and Proclamation* sums up the relationship between the two enterprises that form its title in a telling phrase: "interrelated yet not interchangeable."[13] By this it means to stress that even though the two activities completely interpenetrate in the manner that I have just outlined, the distinction between them remains meaningful, and they do not reduce to the same thing. While evangelization must be done in a spirit of dialogue if it is to be effective, and while dialogue must contain an element of witness if it is to be at all interesting and significant, there remains a crucial difference between them. When one enters into an interreligious encounter intending it to be dialogical, one puts aside the goal of converting the other and attempts to engage in a free interchange with no set goal other than to arrive at new levels of mutual understanding. When one enters into another encounter intending it to be an occasion for proclamation, then one will self-consciously seek to guide the partner to the knowledge and love of Christ. It takes prayer and discernment, and great sensitivity to a host of factors, to know when one or the other intention is the most fitting.

Though the distinction between dialogue and proclamation stands even as each informs and pervades the other, it is now appropriate to ask if these are the only two options for interreligious encounter. Is the need to adjudicate the tension between dialogue and proclamation so pressing that it prevents us from seeing other possibilities?

Perhaps. Let us look at a pair of "ideal type models" of dialogue and proclamation, bearing in mind that these descriptions are solely presented as aids to thought, not as literal descriptions of the real situation. The average educated Christian probably sees proclamation as a kind of sales presentation, where the preacher proclaims the gospel, and the audience hears it and either accepts it or rejects it. There might be some give-and-take that prevents the encounter from devolving into a pure monologue, but in general it follows this dynamic. The same Christian probably sees dialogue as a conversation between equals, where the two share information about their faiths in the interest of learning from each other, establishing a cooperative relationship, or simply striving to live together in peace. What both of these ideal-type models have in common is that they see the "religious traditions" of the participants as static entities insusceptible to change. The Christianity of the evangelist will undergo no modification in the act of proclamation. The faiths shared by participants in the encounter of dialogue will remain as they are, and the participants in dialogue will accomplish no more than to learn about the immutable faith of one another.

Two thousand five hundred years ago, Confucius made the interesting observation that people affect each other in subtle ways simply by coming into proximity with each other and establishing a relationship. Anyone who has been married or made a new friend or joined a new social group is aware, if they reflect on it for a moment, of the adjustments they made in order to establish the new relationships. They did *not* simply remain as they were. Religions behave in much the same way, as a last look at the history with which we began this book will confirm. Jesus' ministry took place largely within the Israelite community of his day, with very few encounters with non-Jews recorded. When he did interact with them, his primary problem was to decide whether or not the God of Israel could have anything to do with non-Israelites. Later, in the Book of Acts, as Christians moved out into broader circles of the known world, they finally broached the question of other religions in a way that we today might recognize. In 1442, when the Roman Catholic establishment had come to believe that all the world had been evangelized and there were no non-Christians, they adopted a tough attitude in the Decree on the Copts. Finally, in our own day, when we know how big the world is and we find we have not been able to convert all its inhabitants in one generation, we see the growth of dialogue with other religions as a mode of relating to them.

More than that, the long-term encounter of Christianity with other religions has produced some effects that perhaps no one planned for or predicted. In a world where Buddhists set up large charity organizations and Sunday schools while Jesuit priests become certified Zen masters and Christian theologians use Buddhist concepts to explicate the Trinity and comment on the Gospel of Mark, something is clearly going on that does not conform to the model of unchanging entities exchanging communications with one another. What we see, rather, is what Paul Ingram called religions in "mutual transformation."[14] As Christianity enters into long-term relationships with other religions, we find it and them adjusting to one another, changing themselves in deep and subtle ways so that they may continue to live together. This does not necessarily imply that as religions continue to exist side by side and interact, the long-term result will be a future convergence—we see that even a man and a woman who have been married more than fifty years retain their individuality, even as they accommodate each other over time.

We can perhaps understand the processes of religious interaction described in the first chapter through the lens of this long-term mutual transformation, which takes place regardless of whether

Christians intend their interactions with other religions to follow the model of dialogue or to follow the model of proclamation. Since only an utter lack of contact can prevent change, Christians in the past employed the strategies of containment, elimination, and expulsion in an attempt to forestall transformation. The polarity of openness versus integrity is, in a very real sense, a response to the inevitability of transformation—"openness" seeing it as an opportunity and welcoming it, "integrity" seeing it as a danger and attempting to hinder it. The important thing to bear in mind is that, regardless of one's theology, the mere fact that religions come into contact *at all* will, in the end, result in changes to all of them. If this is true, then we may expect further transformations in Christianity as it abides in the world of religious diversity.

The question this leaves us with, then, is: Do we trust God to guide the process?

Notes

Introduction: The Religious Scene and the Problem of Diversity

1. Diana L. Eck, *A New Religious America: How a "Christian Country" Has Now Become the World's Most Religiously Diverse Nation* (San Francisco: HarperSanFrancisco, 2001), 1.
2. www.fas.harvard.edu/~pluralsm.

Chapter 1: Sociological and Theoretical Considerations

1. Not all authors share this distinction. Schubert Ogden, for example, defines religion in such a way that humanistic systems may also be included, provided they address the great "existential question" directly. See Schubert M. Ogden, *Is There One True Religion or Are There Many?* (Dallas: Southern Methodist University Press, 1992), 9. I find it more useful to exclude such systems because (1) they do not wish to claim the name *religion* for themselves, because (2) they generally see themselves as opposed to it.
2. Ibid., 7.
3. See Jonathan Z. Smith, , "Religion, Religions, Religious," in *Critical Terms for Religious Studies*, ed. Mark C. Taylor (Chicago: University of Chicago Press, 1998), 269–284.
4. See, for example, Peter Berger, *The Sacred Canopy: Elements of a Sociological Theory of Religion* (Garden City, NY: Doubleday, 1967), chapter 6.
5. Trevor Ling, *The Buddha: Buddhist Civilization in India and Ceylon* (New York: Charles Scribner's Sons, 1976), chapter 2.
6. For the reader who wants to see how different modern Christianity is from the older European Christendom, I suggest reading Alan Watts's *Myth and Ritual in Christianity* (Boston: Beacon Press, 1971), which does an excellent job of evoking what the world looked like to the average person in Europe in the Middle Ages. It paints a worldview where every aspect of life, whether directly connected with religious ritual and belief or not, is understood through the lens of Christianity: "The day is measured by the bells that rung the daily office in the local church or monastery, the planets are pushed through the sky by angels, mental illness is caused by demons, the king holds office because he was appointed

by God, and so on." It is quite illuminating to compare this with the way that even a very religious person today encounters and makes sense of society and the natural world.

7. See Rodney Stark, *The Rise of Christianity: How the Obscure, Marginal Jesus Movement Became the Dominant Religious Force in the Western World in a Few Centuries* (Princeton, NJ: Princeton University Press, 1996), chapter 1.

Chapter 2: Christianity and Other Religions in the Early Period

1. After Alexander's death in 323 BC, the large empire he had conquered quickly fell apart as local generals sought control. Palestine, and especially the southern region and Jerusalem, were hotly disputed between the heirs of Ptolemy in Egypt and the heirs of Seleucus in Syria.

2. For more information, see James C. VanderKam, *An Introduction to Early Judaism* (Grand Rapids, MI: William B. Eerdmans Publishing Company, 2001), 11–32.

3. Ibid., 13–14.

4. Rodney Stark, *The Rise of Christianity: How the Obscure, Marginal Jesus Movement Became the Dominant Religious Force in the Western World in a Few Centuries* (Princeton: Princeton University Press, 1996), *passim*.

5. Ibid., chapter 3.

6. Jacques Dupuis, *Toward a Christian Theology of Religious Pluralism* (Maryknoll, NY: Orbis Books, 1997), 53–54.

7. Justin Martyr, *Second Apology*, XIII, 2–3.

8. Clement of Alexandria, *Stromata* I:5, 3.

9. Francis A. Sullivan, *Salvation Outside the Church? Tracing the History of the Catholic Response* (New York: Paulist Press, 1992); J. P. Theisen, *The Ultimate Church and the Promise of Salvation* (Collegeville, MN: St. John's University Press, 1976); Jacques Dupuis, *Toward a Christian Theology of Religious Pluralism* (Maryknoll, NY: Orbis Books, 1997).

10. Joseph A. DiNoia, *The Diversity of Religions: A Christian Perspective* (Washington, DC: Catholic University of America Press, 1992), 22.

Chapter 3: The Age of Exploration and the European Enlightenment

1. Christopher Columbus, www.moralconcerns.org/past/Amer1492.htm.

2. Jacques Dupuis, *Toward a Christian Theology of Religious Pluralism* (Maryknoll, NY: Orbis Books, 1997), 110*ff*.

3. Specifically, this passage says that Christ went down to preach to those who had not gotten on the Ark with Noah. This image could counter the use of Noah's Ark as a "type" for the Church, a metaphor that, as we saw in the last chapter, was used to affirm that just as only those who boarded

Noah's Ark escaped the flood, so only those who join the Church could escape damnation. This passage seems to indicate that even those who did not get on the boat got a second chance, and so, by extension, even those who do not belong to the Church might still be saved.

4. Dupuis, 117–118.
5. Ibid., 114–116.
6. Ibid., 121–22.
7. Rodney Stark and Roger Finke, "Secularization, R.I.P.," in *Acts of Faith: Explaining the Human Side of Religion* (Berkeley, CA: University of California Press, 2000), 57–82.
8. Jacques Barzun, *From Dawn to Decadence: 500 Years of Western Cultural Life, 1500 to the Present* (New York: HarperCollins, 2000), 4.
9. This represents an interesting history in and of itself. It has been shown by the scholar Lionel Jensen that Confucianism was in fact much more "religious" than the Europeans had been led to believe. The Jesuit missionaries in China, realizing that Confucian practices and values were so deeply entrenched in Chinese culture that it would be futile to try and replace them entirely with Christianity, tried to show that such practices as ancestor veneration were not "religious" at all, which would mean that they did not contradict Christianity. If Chinese converts could still be allowed to participate in ancestral rites, they would be much more likely to convert. Thus, Jesuit writings about Chinese culture, which for a couple of centuries were the sole source of information about Chinese religion for the European intelligentsia, deliberately portrayed it as a set of secular civic and familial practices, and omitted mention of such things as animal sacrifices in Confucian temples. Ironically, then, it was the writings of missionaries that gave the secularists in Europe the idea that Confucianism represented a real alternative to the religious state. See Lionel Jensen, *Manufacturing Confucianism: Chinese Traditions and Universal Civilization* (Durham: Duke University Press, 1997).
10. Both these passages are cited in Jonathan Z. Smith, "Religion, Religions, Religious," in *Critical Terms for Religious Studies*, ed. Mark C. Taylor (Chicago: University of Chicago Press, 1998), 269.
11. See David Hume, *The Natural History of Religion*, ed. H. E. Root (Palo Alto: Stanford University Press, 1957).
12. For a readable introduction to these theorists, see Daniel L. Pals, *Seven Theories of Religion* (Oxford, England: Oxford University Press, 1996).
13. Thomas Goldstein, *Dawn of Modern Science: From the Arabs to Leonardo da Vinci* (Boston: Houghton Mifflin, 1980), 76.
14. See James A. Wiseman, *Theology and Modern Science: Quest for Coherence* (New York: Continuum, 2002), chapter 1, for more historical background.

15. Quoted in ibid., 16.
16. Barzun, 507–508.
17. Spinoza was ahead of his time in proposing such a universal World-Spirit, and in the century and a half between him and Schleiermacher, to be called a "Spinozist" was a reproach. It meant that one was an uncritical pantheist and a non-Christian. Schleiermacher decried Christendom's spurning of the man he called the "holy, rejected Spinoza." Friedrich Schleiermacher, *On Religion: Speeches to Its Cultured Despisers*, trans. John Oman (New York: Harper and Row, 1958), 40.
18. Ibid., 44, italics added.
19. Barzun, 471–2.
20. Jonathan Z. Smith, "Religion, Religions, Religious," in *Critical Terms for Religious Studies*, Mark C. Taylor, ed. (Chicago: University of Chicago Press, 1988), 271.

Chapter 4: New Developments in the Modern Period

1. This is not something that one ought to take for granted. Historically, only three pre-nineteenth-century religions have been missionary from their founding: Buddhism, Christianity, and Islam. Other religions generally do not seek to convert others.
2. Missionaries seem to have realized this. In my own research into missionary efforts in Taiwan (mostly Presbyterian), I have often been struck at the way in which missionaries, upon disembarking at the port of Tamsui, walked right past the Chinese city dwellers and headed directly into the mountains where the aboriginal tribes lived, so that most Christians in Taiwan today are to be found among these tribes rather than among the Han Chinese.
3. See Kitsiri Malalgoda, *Buddhism in Sinhalese Society 1750–1900: A Study of Religious Revival and Change* (Berkeley, CA: University of California Press, 1976), 191–255.
4. See Charles B. Jones, *Buddhism in Taiwan: Religion and the State 1660–1990* (Honolulu, HI: University of Hawaii Press, 1999), 198–217.
5. John R. Mott, "The Evangelization of the World in This Generation" (www.abcog.org/mott5.htm, 1944).
6. Charles Clayton Morrison, "The World Missionary Conference, 1910," in *The Christian Century* (July 4–11, 1974), 660.
7. The word *syncretism* refers to the uncritical and unsystematic blending together of elements from several religions.
8. See Rick Fields, *How the Swans Came to the Lake: A Narrative History of Buddhism in America* (Boston: Shambhala Publications, 1992), 35–53, for more on Jones.

9. Wilfred Cantwell Smith, "Scripture as Form and Content: Their Emergence in the Western World," in *Rethinking Scripture: Essays from a Comparative Perspective*, ed. Miriam Levering (Albany, NY: State University of New York Press, 1989), 33–34.

10. Fields, 39–40, 55.

11. Ibid., 61.

12. Ibid., 152.

13. Ibid., 120–121.

14. Diana L. Eck, *A New Religious America: How a "Christian Country" Has Now Become the World's Most Religiously Diverse Nation* (San Francisco: HarperSanFrancisco, 2001), 96–104.

15. Fields, 337.

16. Helen Tworkov, *Zen in America: Profiles of Five Teachers* (San Francisco: North Point Press, 1989), 224–225.

17. Eck, 239–243.

18. Fields, 71.

19. Will Herberg, *Protestant-Catholic-Jew: An Essay in American Religious Sociology* (Chicago: University of Chicago Press, 1983), 29*ff.*

20. www.ncpa.org.

21. See www.pluralism.org/resources/statistics/tradition.php; see also Eck, 2–3.

22. Martin Baumann, "Global Buddhism: Developmental Periods, Regional Histories, and a New Analytical Perspective," in *Journal of Global Buddhism* (www.globalbuddhism.org, vol. 2, 2001), 1.

23. Jacques Dupuis, *Toward a Christian Theology of Religious Pluralism* (Maryknoll, NY: Orbis Books, 1997), 133–143.

24. This phrase refers to an ignorance of the Christian gospel for reasons the individual cannot overcome, either due to mental deficiency or historical circumstance. Thus, it could be claimed that the natives of North and South America were "invincibly ignorant" of the gospel prior to the discovery of the New World, and so could not be held responsible for not belonging to the Church.

25. The official name of this text is "Declaration on the Relation of the Church to Non-Christian Religions." Vatican documents are usually referred to by the first phrase of the Latin text, in this case, the phrase, "In our time . . ." (*Nostra Aetate*).

26. *Nostra Aetate* (www.vatican.va, 1965), §2.

27. Christians are sometimes surprised to discover that the Qur'an affirms Jesus' virgin birth, and there have been Muslims that practiced Marian devotions.

28. *Nostra Aetate*, §4.

29. *Ex Corde Ecclesia* (www.vatican.va, 1990), §47. Byron L. Sherwin and
    Harold Kasimow, ed., *John Paul II and Interreligious Dialogue* (Mary-
    knoll, NY: Orbis Books, 1999) is a very good source for Pope John Paul
    II's activities and pronouncements regarding interreligious dialogue, as
    well as for responses from leaders of other religions to his efforts.

30. *Dialogue and Proclamation* (www.vatican.va, 1991), §74; reproduced in-
    Francesco Gioia, ed., *Interreligious Dialogue: The Official Teaching of the
    Catholic Church (1963–1995)* (Boston: Pauline Books and Media, 1994),
    636.

31. *Dominus Iesus* (www.vatican.va, 2000), §22.

32. Ibid.

33. George M. Marsden, *Fundamentalism and American Culture: The Shap-
    ing of Twentieth-Century Evangelicalism 1870–1925* (New York: Oxford
    University Press, 1980), 118.

34. www.xmission.com/~fidelis/volume4/chapter2/burrell.html.

35. Marsden, 120.

36. Paul F. Knitter, *No Other Name? A Critical Survey of Christian Attitudes
    Toward the World Religions* (Maryknoll, NY: Orbis Books, 1985), 84.

37. See Gerald R. McDermott, *Can Evangelicals Learn from World Religions?:
    Jesus, Revelation, and Religious Traditions* (Downer's Grove, IL: Inter-
    Varsity Press, 2000), 30–31, for a statement of the evangelical position
    of the supremacy of scripture.

38. Schubert M. Ogden, *Is There One True Religion or Are There Many?* (Dal-
    las: Southern Methodist University Press, 1992), 40–51.

39. Ibid., 50.

40. Ibid., 83.

41. David Lochhead, *The Dialogical Imperative: A Christian Reflection on In-
    terfaith Encounter* (Maryknoll, NY: Orbis Books, 1988), 35–39.

42. This, and all other resolutions of the Lambeth Conferences, may be
    found at www.lambethconference.org.

43. Leonard Swidler and Seiichi Yagi, *A Bridge to Buddhist-Christian Dia-
    logue* (Mahwah, NJ: Paulist Press, 1988).

44. John P. Keenan, *The Meaning of Christ: A Mahayana Theology* (Mary-
    knoll, NY: Orbis Books, 1989).

45. John P. Keenan, *The Gospel of Mark: A Mahayana Reading* (Maryknoll,
    NY: Orbis Books, 1995).

46. Francis X. Clooney, *Hindu Wisdom for All God's Children* (Maryknoll,
    NY: Orbis Books, 1998).

Chapter 5: Current Theological Models

1. For an example, see Gerald R. McDermott, *Can Evangelicals Learn From World Religions?: Jesus, Revelation, and Religious Traditions* (Downer's Grove, IL: InterVarsity Press, 2000), 30–31.

2. Lausanne Covenant (www.gospelcom.net/lcwe/statements/covenant .html, 1974).

3. Holmes Welch, The Buddhist Revival in China (Harvard East Asian Studies, 33) (Cambridge, MA: Harvard University Press, 1968), 240–241.

4. Galen Amstutz, *Interpreting Amida: History and Orientalism in the Study of Pure Land Buddhism* (Albany, NY: State University of New York Press, 1997), chapters 3–5.

5. Kenneth Boa, *Cults, World Religions, and You* (Wheaton, IL: Victor Books, 1984).

6. C. S. Lewis, *The Last Battle* (New York: HarperTrophy, 1994), 201–206.

7. *Dominus Iesus* (www.vatican.va, 2000), §21.

8. John Hick, *An Interpretation of Religion: Human Responses to the Transcendent* (New Haven, CT: Yale University Press, 1989); John Hick, *A Christian Theology of Religions: The Rainbow of Faiths* (Louisville, KY: Westminster John Knox Press, 1995). This may, in a way, seem very similar to the position of Schleiermacher that we encountered in chapter three. Two differences are worth noting, however. First, Schleiermacher had far less information about Asian religions than does Hick, and so the former's "World-Spirit" looks much more like the Western God than does Hick's Real. Second, Schleiermacher still very much believed in the superiority of Christianity in reflecting this World-Spirit, and so he would be better understood as an inclusivist, albeit of the most liberal type, than as a pluralist.

9. S. Mark Heim, *Salvations: Truth and Difference in Religion* (Maryknoll, NY: Orbis Books, 1997), 36, 138.

10. One may see, for example, Robert Gimello's articles about the Buddha's enlightenment wherein he demonstrates quite conclusively that the Buddha actually achieved and then rejected the mystical vision sought by other religious figures of his day, and proceeded to have a mystical experience of a very different sort. See Robert M. Gimello, "Mysticism and Meditation," in *Mysticism and Philosophical Analysis*, ed. Steven T. Katz (New York: Oxford University Press, 1978); Robert M. Gimello, "Mysticisms in Their Contexts," in *Mysticism and Religious Traditions*, ed. Steven T. Katz (New York: Oxford University Press, 1983).

11. Heim, p. 137.

12. Some readers may be familiar with another recent attempt to fashion a parallelist approach to religious diversity: Stephen Kaplan's *Different*

Paths, Different Summits: A Model for Religious Pluralism (Lanham, MD: Rowman and Littlefield, 2002). Although the title of the book and the author's intentions seem to indicate a parallelist approach, I have not dealt with it in this section for a couple of reasons: (1) Kaplan's argument is based on an extended analogy with holography, and to understand it requires a lengthy explanation of holographic film and projection techniques; and (2) Kaplan specifically brackets out any consideration of the salvific efficacy of other religions, and so is not espousing any theological position. This puts his discussion outside our topic.

Chapter 6: Balancing Dialogue and Mission

1. *Dialogue and Proclamation* (www.vatican.va, 1991), §42.
2. *Monastic Interreligious Dialogue Bulletin*, ed. James Wiseman, OSB (72: May 2004), 2.
3. See for example Robert E. Kennedy, *Zen Spirit, Christian Spirit: The Place of Zen in Christian Life* (New York: Continuum, 1996); and Anthony de Mello, *Sadhana: A Way to God* (New York: HarperCollins, 1983) for just two of the many books that have appeared.
4. An *ashram* is a place in Indian religion where students live together with a teacher for spiritual instruction and practice.
5. Harvey Cox, *Many Mansions: A Christian's Encounter with Other Faiths* (Boston: Beacon Press, 1988), 8.
6. Holmes Welch, *The Buddhist Revival in China* (Harvard East Asian Studies, 33) (Cambridge, MA: Harvard University Press, 1968), 224–225.
7. *Dialogue and Proclamation*, §79.
8. Leonard Swidler and Seiichi Yagi, *A Bridge to Buddhist-Christian Dialogue* (Mahwah, NJ: Paulist Press, 1988), 1.
9. For example, a book I received from a visiting Saudi Arabian delegation on Muslim-Christian dialogue consisted of a series of transcripts of dialogues between several Muslim leaders and two Arab Christian ministers in the Sudanese capital, Khartoum, shortly after the Islamic revolution there. The dialogues end with both ministers converting to Islam, although the circumstances of their conversion might seem very suspect to Western Christian readers. See IIASA (Institute of Islamic and Arabic Sciences in America), *Dialogue Between Islam and Christianity* (Fairfax, VA: IIASA, 1999).
10. John E. Wills, Jr., "The Seventeenth-Century Transformation: Taiwan Under the Dutch and the Cheng Regime," in *Taiwan: A New History*, ed. Murray A. Rubinstein (Armonk, NY: M. E. Sharpe, 1999), 91–92.
11. See Swidler and Yagi, 5–7.
12. Rodney Stark, *The Rise of Christianity: How the Obscure, Marginal Jesus*

Movement Became the Dominant Religious Force in the Western World in a Few Centuries (Princeton, NJ: Princeton University Press, 1996), 20–21.

13. *Dialogue and Proclamation,* §77.

14. Paul O. Ingram, *The Modern Buddhist-Christian Dialogue: Two Universalistic Religions in Transformation* (Studies in Comparative Religion, vol. 2) (Lewiston, NY: Edwin Mellen Press, 1988).

Selected Bibliography

Amstutz, Galen. *Interpreting Amida: History and Orientalism in the Study of Pure Land Buddhism.* Albany, NY: State University of New York Press, 1997.

Ariarajah, S. Wesley. "Dialogue, Interfaith." In *The Dictionary of the Ecumenical Movement,* edited by Geoffrey Wainwright et al. Grand Rapids, MI: William B. Eerdmans Publishing Company, 1991.

Barzun, Jacques. *From Dawn to Decadence: 500 Years of Western Cultural Life, 1500 to the Present.* New York: HarperCollins, 2000.

Baumann, Martin. "Global Buddhism: Developmental Periods, Regional Histories, and a New Analytical Perspective." In *Journal of Global Buddhism,* www.globalbuddhism.org, volume 2, 2001, 1–43.

Berger, Peter. *The Sacred Canopy: Elements of a Sociological Theory of Religion.* Garden City, NY: Doubleday, 1967.

Boa, Kenneth. *Cults, World Religions, and You.* Wheaton, IL: Victor Books, 1984.

Clement of Alexandria. *Stromata* I:5.

Clooney, Francis X. *Hindu Wisdom for All God's Children.* Maryknoll, NY: Orbis Books, 1998.

Columbus, Christopher. www.moralconcerns.org/past/Amer1492.htm.

Cox, Harvey. *Many Mansions: A Christian's Encounter with Other Faiths.* Boston: Beacon Press, 1988.

de Mello, Anthony. *Sadhana: A Way to God.* New York: HarperCollins, 1983.

Dialogue and Proclamation. www.vatican.va, 1991.

DiNoia, Joseph A. *The Diversity of Religions: A Christian Perspective.* Washington, DC: Catholic University of America Press, 1992.

Dominus Iesus. www.vatican.va, 2000.

Dupuis, Jacques. *Toward a Christian Theology of Religious Pluralism.* Maryknoll, NY: Orbis Books, 1997.

Eck, Diana L. *A New Religious America: How a "Christian Country" Has Now Become the World's Most Religiously Diverse Nation.* San Francisco: HarperSanFrancisco, 2001.

Ex Corde Ecclesia. www.vatican.va, 1990.

Fields, Rick. *How the Swans Came to the Lake: A Narrative History of Buddhism in America.* Boston: Shambhala Publications, 1992.

Gimello, Robert M. "Mysticism and Meditation." In *Mysticism and Philosophical Analysis,* edited by Steven T. Katz. New York: Oxford University Press, 1978.

———. "Mysticisms in Their Contexts." In *Mysticism and Religious Traditions,* edited by Steven T. Katz. New York: Oxford University Press, 1983.

Gioia, Francesco, ed. *Interreligious Dialogue: The Official Teaching of the Catholic Church, 1963–1995.* Boston: Pauline Books and Media, 1994.

Goldstein, Thomas. *Dawn of Modern Science: From the Arabs to Leonardo da Vinci.* Boston: Houghton Mifflin, 1980.

Heim, S. Mark. *Salvations: Truth and Difference in Religion.* Maryknoll, NY: Orbis Books, 1997.

Herberg, Will. *Protestant-Catholic-Jew: An Essay in American Religious Sociology.* Chicago: University of Chicago Press, 1983.

Hick, John. *A Christian Theology of Religions: The Rainbow of Faiths.* Louisville, KY: Westminster John Knox Press, 1995.

———. *An Interpretation of Religion: Human Responses to the Transcendent.* New Haven, CT: Yale University Press, 1989.

Hume, David. *The Natural History of Religion,* edited by H. E. Root. Palo Alto, CA: Stanford University Press, 1957.

IIASA (Institute of Islamic and Arabic Sciences in America). *Dialogue Between Islam and Christianity.* Fairfax, VA: IIASA, 1999.

Ingram, Paul O. *The Modern Buddhist-Christian Dialogue: Two Universalistic Religions in Transformation.* Studies in Comparative Religion, volume 2. Lewiston, NY: Edwin Mellen Press, 1988.

Jensen, Lionel. *Manufacturing Confucianism: Chinese Traditions and Universal Civilization.* Durham, NC: Duke University Press, 1997.

Jones, Charles B. *Buddhism in Taiwan: Religion and the State 1660–1990.* Honolulu: University of Hawaii Press, 1999.

Justin Martyr, *Second Apology,* XIII.

Kaplan, Stephen. *Different Paths, Different Summits: A Model for Religious Pluralism.* Lanham, MD: Rowman and Littlefield, 2002.

Keenan, John P. *The Gospel of Mark: A Mahayana Reading.* Maryknoll, NY: Orbis Books, 1995.

———. *The Meaning of Christ: A Mahayana Theology.* Maryknoll, NY: Orbis Books, 1989.

Kennedy, Robert E. *Zen Spirit, Christian Spirit: The Place of Zen in Christian Life.* New York: Continuum, 1996.

Knitter, Paul F. *No Other Name? A Critical Survey of Christian Attitudes Toward the World Religions.* Maryknoll, NY: Orbis Books, 1985.

Lambeth Conference Archives, www.lambethconference.org.

Lausanne Covenant, www.gospelcom.net/lcwe/statements/covenant.html, 1974.

Lewis, C. S. *The Last Battle.* New York: HarperTrophy, 1994.

Ling, Trevor. *The Buddha: Buddhist Civilization in India and Ceylon.* New York: Charles Scribner's Sons, 1976.

Lochhead, David. *The Dialogical Imperative: A Christian Reflection on Interfaith Encounter.* Maryknoll, NY: Orbis Books, 1988.

Malalgoda, Kitsiri. *Buddhism in Sinhalese Society 1750–1900: A Study of Religious Revival and Change.* Berkeley, CA: University of California Press, 1976.

Marsden, George M. *Fundamentalism and American Culture: The Shaping of Twentieth-Century Evangelicalism 1870–1925.* New York: Oxford University Press, 1980.

McDermott, Gerald R. *Can Evangelicals Learn from World Religions?: Jesus, Revelation, and Religious Traditions.* Downer's Grove, IL: InterVarsity Press, 2000.

Morrison, Charles Clayton. "The World Missionary Conference, 1910." In *The Christian Century*, July 4–11, 1974, 660.

Mott, John R. "The Evangelization of the World in This Generation," www.abcog.org/mott5.htm,1944.

Nostra Aetate (Document of Second Vatican Council), www.vatican.va, 1965.

Ogden, Schubert M. *Is There One True Religion or Are There Many?* Dallas: Southern Methodist University Press, 1992.

Pals, Daniel L. *Seven Theories of Religion.* Oxford, England: Oxford University Press, 1996.

Preus, J. Samuel. *Explaining Religion: Criticism and Theory from Bodin to Freud.* New Haven, CT: Yale University Press, 1987.

Raboteau, Albert. *Slave Religion: The "Invisible Institution" in the Antebellum South.* New York: Oxford University Press, 1978.

Schleiermacher, Friedrich. *On Religion: Speeches to Its Cultured Despisers,* translated by John Oman. New York: Harper and Row, 1958.

Sherwin, Byron L., and Harold Kasimow, eds. *John Paul II and Interreligious Dialogue.* Maryknoll, NY: Orbis Books, 1999.

Smith, Jonathan Z. "Religion, Religions, Religious." In *Critical Terms for Religious Studies,* edited by Mark C. Taylor. Chicago: University of Chicago Press, 1998, 269–284.

Smith, Wilfred Cantwell. "Scripture as Form and Content: Their Emergence in the Western World." In *Rethinking Scripture: Essays from a Comparative Perspective,* edited by Miriam Levering. Albany, NY: State University of New York Press, 1989, 29–57.

Stark, Rodney. *The Rise of Christianity: How the Obscure, Marginal Jesus Movement Became the Dominant Religious Force in the Western World in a Few Centuries.* Princeton, NJ: Princeton University Press, 1996.

Stark, Rodney, and Roger Finke. *Acts of Faith: Explaining the Human Side of Religion.* Berkeley, CA: University of California Press, 2000.

Sullivan, Francis A. *Salvation Outside the Church? Tracing the History of the Catholic Response.* New York: Paulist Press, 1992.

Swidler, Leonard, and Seiichi Yagi. *A Bridge to Buddhist-Christian Dialogue.* Mahwah, NJ: Paulist Press, 1988.

Theisen, J. P. *The Ultimate Church and the Promise of Salvation.* Collegeville, MN: St. John's University Press, 1976.

Tworkov, Helen. *Zen in America: Profiles of Five Teachers.* San Francisco: North Point Press, 1989.

VanderKam, James C. *An Introduction to Early Judaism.* Grand Rapids, MI: William B. Eerdmans Publishing Company, 2001.

Wagner, Roy. *The Invention of Culture.* Chicago: University of Chicago Press, 1975.

Watts, Alan. *Myth and Ritual in Christianity.* Boston: Beacon Press, 1971.

Welch, Holmes. *The Buddhist Revival in China.* Harvard East Asian Studies, 33. Cambridge, MA: Harvard University Press, 1968.

Wills, John E., Jr. "The Seventeenth-Century Transformation: Taiwan Under the Dutch and the Cheng Regime." In *Taiwan: A New History,* edited by Murray A. Rubinstein. Armonk, NY: M. E. Sharpe, 1999, 84–106.

Wiseman, James A. *Theology and Modern Science: Quest for Coherence.* New York: Continuum, 2002.

Church Documents on the Internet:

Roman Catholic official documents may be found at: www.vatican.va

Lambeth Conference resolutions may be found at: www.lambethconference.org

World Council of Churches Interreligious Relations and Dialogue Web site: www.wcc-coe.org/wcc/what/interreligious/index-e.html